Faith to Follow

THE JOURNEY OF BECOMING A PASTOR'S WIFE

KATE MEADOWS

WESTBOW
PRESS®
A DIVISION OF THOMAS NELSON
& ZONDERVAN

WestBow Press books may be ordered through booksellers or by contacting:

WestBow Press
A Division of Thomas Nelson & Zondervan
1663 Liberty Drive
Bloomington, IN 47403
www.westbowpress.com
844-714-3454

Because of the dynamic nature of the Internet, any web addresses or
links contained in this book may have changed since publication and
may no longer be valid. The views expressed in this work are solely those
of the author and do not necessarily reflect the views of the publisher,
and the publisher hereby disclaims any responsibility for them.

Any people depicted in stock imagery provided by Getty Images are
models, and such images are being used for illustrative purposes only.
Certain stock imagery © Getty Images.

All Scripture quotations, unless otherwise indicated, are taken from
the Holy Bible, New International Version®, NIV®. Copyright ©1973,
1978, 1984, 2011 by Biblica, Inc.® Used by permission of Zondervan.
All rights reserved worldwide. www.zondervan.com The "NIV"
and "New International Version" are trademarks registered in the
United States Patent and Trademark Office by Biblica, Inc.®

Scripture quotations marked (ESV) are from The ESV® Bible (The Holy Bible,
English Standard Version®), copyright © 2001 by Crossway, a publishing
ministry of Good News Publishers. Used by permission. All rights reserved.

ISBN: 978-1-6642-0579-6 (sc)
ISBN: 978-1-6642-0578-9 (hc)
ISBN: 978-1-6642-0789-9 (e)

Library of Congress Control Number: 2020919265

Print information available on the last page.

WestBow Press rev. date: 11/16/2020

CONTENTS

Dedication ix
Acknowledgments xi
Introduction xiii

PART 1: THE DECISION 1
Chapter 1: Wrestling with God through the Decision 3
Chapter 2: Community in the Decision 10
Chapter 3: Contentment and Sacrifice in the Decision 15
Four Ways to Prepare for Seminary 21
Chapter 4: Faith in Your Role in the Decision 25
Health Insurance: The Concordia Plan or
Something Else? 29

PART 2: LIFE AT SEMINARY 33
Chapter 5: Wrestling with God at the Seminary 35
The Seminary Wife's Call to Church Work 38
Deaconess and DCE: What's the Difference? 48
Chapter 6: Community at the Seminary 50
Four Ways to Earn Extra Cash at the Seminary 55
Resident Field Education: Moments of Practice for
Ministry 59
Chapter 7: Contentment and Sacrifice at the Seminary 62
Women's Formation at the Seminary: How do We
Grow in Faith Alongside Our Husbands? 68

Chapter 8: Faith in Your Role at the Seminary............................75
    Six Ways to Help Kids Connect.....................................84

INTERLUDE: A BRIEF HISTORY OF SEMINARY 89

PART 3: VICARAGE AND THE CALL PROCESS........... 109
Chapter 9: Vicarage – A Bird's Eye View 111
Chapter 10: Getting Involved on Vicarage................................120
    When Receiving Gifts is a Burden 125
Chapter 11: From Vicarage to Call...129
Chapter 12: Identity in the Call Process....................................137

PART 4: TRANSITION FROM THE CALL TO THE
**   CHURCH...151**
Chapter 13: Wrestling with God AFTER the Call....................153
Chapter 14: Community in the Church 165
    Seven Ways to Make Connections........................... 174
Chapter 15: Contentment and Sacrifice in the Church.............177
Chapter 16: Faith in Your Role in the Church...........................191

Study Guide Questions..203
    Chapter 1: Wrestling With God Through the Decision.....203
    Chapter 2: Community in the Decision 203
    Chapter 3: Contentment and Sacrifice in the Decision..... 204
    Chapter 4: Faith in Your Role Through the Decision 205
    Chapter 5: Wrestling With God at Seminary..................... 205
    Chapter 6: Community at Seminary 206
    Chapter 7: Contentment and Sacrifice at Seminary 207
    Chapter 8: Faith in Your Role at Seminary........................ 208
    Chapter 9: Vicarage: A Bird's Eye View 209
    Chapter 10: Getting Involved on Vicarage........................210
    Chapter 11: From Vicarage to Call....................................210
    Chapter 12: Identity in the Call Process............................211
    Chapter 13: Wrestling With God After the Call................212

Chapter 14: Community in the Church 213
Chapter 15: Contentment and Sacrifice in the Church......213
Chapter 16: Faith in Your Role as a Pastor's Wife...............214

Bibliography...217
Index 219
About the Author 223

DEDICATION

This book is dedicated to the women who support their husbands in ministry and who courageously step out in faith, even if there's only enough light to see one step ahead.

> *And we know that for those who love God all things work together for good, for those who are called according to his purpose. -Romans 8:28*

ACKNOWLEDGMENTS

All thanks and praise to God for opening the doors to this book project. He has guided my every step, even the mucky ones! Many times I prayed for Him to show me the way through. I even prayed that He would put road blocks in my path, if He did not want this project to happen.

He never put up road blocks.

I am so thankful to the dozens of women who wholeheartedly and courageously shared pieces of their lives with me for this book. For all of the coffee dates, meetings in apartments and one-on-one connections in my home, thank you. If you responded to my incessant questions on Facebook or via email, thank you. Thank you for your patience, your wisdom, your insight. Most of all, thank you for your willingness to share your experience, and for your compassion and desire to support the women who come after us.

Thank you to the staff, faculty members and wives of faculty at Concordia Theological Seminary and Concordia Seminary for your extended time and insight on subject matters I was less familiar with: Dr. Gerhard Bode for help and generosity with historical expertise; Dr. Tim Saleska and Celina Haupt for facts about ministerial formation and women's formation at Concordia Seminary; Dr. Gary Zieroth and Sara Pulse for ongoing dialogue about connecting the book with readers at Concordia Theological Seminary; Renee Gibbs for her longstanding connections to women at the seminary; and Katie Nafzger for ongoing dialogue about incorporating the book into a women's curriculum at

Concordia Seminary. Special thanks to the Concordia Historical Institute staff for helping me access pertinent information.

I am indebted to the eight beta readers who agreed to read and offer feedback on the book's first draft: Jenny Price, Carrie Holder, Renee Lehr, Renee Gibbs, Katie Nafzger, Celina Haupt, Jan Meadows, and Ruth Neely. Jenny, thank you for holding me to task and challenging me to go deeper. Carrie, thank you for catching small errors and questioning parts that didn't click. Renee L., thank you for your tireless encouragement and excitement and candid conversations about life as a pastor's wife. Renee G., thank you for your love and compassion and endless encouragement, and for being such a model of perseverance. Katie, thank you for your openness and for thinking outside the box with me. Celina, thank you for your excitement, encouragement and insight that helped to inform the book's direction. Jan, thank you for being my rock through this, the one I could depend on for quick turnaround, for sharing pieces of your own journey as a pastor's wife with me as you read. Thank you to you and Phil for raising an amazing man I am proud to call my husband. And Mom (Ruth), thank you for the many late nights that you sat with the book's chapters and for your unending belief in me and my crazy ambitions. You are each strong women of God that keep me standing in awe. You amaze me.

Finally, thank you for my family – husband Bryan and sons Will and Eli – for life together. Bryan, you patiently listened as I read every chapter aloud. You critiqued each chapter with care and thoughtfulness, and you did not let me give up. Thank you. I love you. And Will and Eli, you are my lights, reminding me to smile and laugh and not sweat the small stuff. I love you to the moon and back.

INTRODUCTION

As my husband, Bryan, and I prepared to move to St. Louis where he would begin his theological studies at Concordia Seminary in the fall of 2015, I longed for a road map. Seminary had been in the back of his mind for years, but fear had always held him back. Was it not crazy to walk away from a steady job that financially took care of his family, which included two little boys? Wouldn't the stigma of being a "PK" (pastor's kid) reap negative results on our children's own walks of faith? What if his family – kids and wife – came to resent church, because it was always competing for his time and attention?

But the desire to become a pastor persisted. At Le Fou Frog in Kansas City, where we were celebrating our seventh wedding anniversary, Bryan asked me what I thought about the possibility of him applying for seminary. We both knew, at least from a distant perspective, what seminary meant. It meant he would leave a steady job that kept our family comfortable financially. It meant not just one major move to seminary, but multiple moves down the road. The traditional path to becoming a pastor in our denomination, the Lutheran Church-Missouri Synod (LCMS), is a wild string of transitions. It consists of two years on a seminary campus in St. Louis, Missouri, or Fort Wayne, Indiana, followed by one year of pastoral internship (called vicarage) at an LCMS church anywhere in the country (as assigned by a placement director), and a final year back on campus[1]. Once a student earns his Master of Divinity (M-Div) degree, he is eligible to receive his first call[2]; and again, it can be to any LCMS church in the country.

In our seven years of marriage, we had already moved five times and had lived in four states. Bryan and I were both tired of living in a "temporary" status wherever we were. Seminary would mean another four years of "temporary," and then most likely starting over in yet another new place.

It also meant I would have to walk away from what was for me an ideal work-life balance. For four years I had wrestled mightily with how to live out my role as "mom" first and foremost, without completely shedding my identity as a working professional. How can we most fully live in the roles to which God calls us when He calls us to multiple roles? Constantly wrestling with that question was hard enough in Kansas City, where we were at least somewhat stable and had good friends and a solid church home. How would my roles change if we moved to St. Louis – a place where we knew no one – and then to who-knows-where? Furthermore, how would such a drastic life change in our family affect our boys, neither of whom were yet in Kindergarten?

At the restaurant, I stared at Bryan from across the table. I wasn't ready to answer his question about seminary. I needed a moment. I stood up, said I had to use the restroom, and booked it across the restaurant to the door marked "*FILLE.*" There was

---

[1] The traditional route through seminary is via this four-year Master of Divinity program. However, in effort to accommodate more pastors and families, the LCMS has in the last decade outlined alternative paths to becoming a pastor. This book focuses primarily on the traditional M-Div route, but women whose husbands/fiancés are considering/completing an alternative option will also encounter many of the struggles, questions and joys outlined in this book.

[2] Most students in an LCMS seminary take a first Call as soon as they are eligible. However, some continue with their studies to pursue further degrees.

a bright painting on the wall in the bathroom, and I remember staring hard at it, wanting to punch it for its simplicity and beauty.

Why? I asked in a huffed whisper, as I tapped my head against the wall.

It's not that I didn't want my husband to go to seminary. I would be his No. 1 cheerleader on his quest to become a pastor. I had recognized his heart for ministry long before he had. Many other people saw it, too. Every once in a while at a family gathering, his dad would lean over to me and whisper, "You know, I could see him becoming a pastor someday." More than once my mom had asked me if I thought Bryan might ever be a pastor. People saw that warmth and drive in him, and his penchant to go deep with theological issues.

My turmoil was in the timing. Why *now*? Why now, when I had finally found what for me was the perfect balance of writing and teaching, family and being a stay-at-home mom? Why now, when we were in the middle of raising two kids? Why now, when we were finally growing comfortable in the community we lived in?

A big part of me wanted to say no to seminary. The thought of what we would have to give up as a family for Bryan to go back to school full time overwhelmed me. Money. Job. Move. Questions and questions and more questions.

But God is bigger than all of that. He was certainly bigger than me. I knew His timing was greater than my timing. Who was *I* to say "no" to God? If He had indeed put the calling on Bryan's heart to become a pastor, I wasn't about to get in the way.

I walked back out to our table and tried to smile. *Yes,* I said to my husband, *we can do this.*

How?

I had no idea.

But I knew that if God was leading us, He would carry us through.

How does a family make life at seminary, and later, life in full time public ministry, work? More pointedly, how do the women who come with these men to seminary continue to seek or pursue their God-given vocations as wives, mothers, and/or working professionals? These are the two big questions that lived in me prior to and during our seminary experience. Most men who pursue an M-Div at an LCMS seminary have a well paved road ahead of them: First-year classes, second-year classes, vicarage, fourth-year classes, first call. The women who come with these men don't. Until roughly the 1960s, men pursued a seminary education through the LCMS on their own, without women and families in tow. But within the last sixty years, the landscape of seminary in the LCMS has changed dramatically. Now, roughly half of the men at Concordia Seminary are married, and about twenty-five percent have children. In St. Louis, fifty-three percent are considered second-career students, while thirty percent are second-career in Fort Wayne[3].

As my husband started attending classes and our family encountered other people at the seminary, I realized that these colossal questions were not mine alone. Every family we met was facing these questions in their own way. What did these families look like? There was no cookie-cutter mold.

At any given time, the seminary communities in both St. Louis and Fort Wayne include:

- Young, single men who came straight through the Concordia universities system
- Men who are newly married
- M-Div students who are dating or married to deaconess students
- Young families with stay-at-home moms

---

[3] Second-career refers to men who have left one career to pursue another career as a pastor. Statistics provided by Admissions departments on both seminary campuses, as well as numbers published in the November 2019 issue of *The Lutheran Witness*.

- Young families with moms who work outside the home
- "Second career" families
- Couples without children
- Couples who are trying to have children
- Pregnant women
- New moms
- Retired couples
- Grandparents

The diversity of the seminary population doesn't stop there. Men have left careers in accounting, architecture, engineering, television broadcasting, farming, restaurant managing, graphic design, teaching to pursue a ministerial degree. Some are lifelong Lutherans, but many aren't. Some are former Catholics. Others come from Nazarene, Mennonite, Jehovah's Witness and even atheist backgrounds.

The tremendous diversity of age, life experience, and geographical and religious upbringing made one thing clear: There is no "right" way or "one" way for a family to go through seminary. But as I started to meet women whose husbands or fiancés were in seminary, I learned that many of us ask the same questions prior to, throughout and even after the seminary journey: "Who am I in this process?" and "Where do I fit?"

Like the men, the women, too, come from a wide variety of backgrounds. Teachers. Biologists. Mothers. Homemakers. Speech pathologists. Writers. Childcare providers. DCEs and Deaconesses. Kara Johnson left a beloved job as a graphic designer in Nebraska to come to seminary with her husband. Rachel Warner was enjoying a solid career as an architect in St. Louis when she met her future husband, Daniel, a seminary student. Rachell Highley was planning to enroll in the seminary's deaconess program when she met her husband, Joseph, a seminary student.

I thought there must be a book or some sort of resource that outlined how women and families thrive during the seminary years alongside husbands and fathers. After all, the process of preparing to become a pastor's wife is a critical and sacred journey – and a plight that most of us aren't exactly prepared for. Only eight percent of the women who responded to a survey for this book reported they had always imagined they would one day be a pastor's wife. Resources exist for pastors' wives[4]. However, most resources I found were outdated and broad-based and not centered on the unique LCMS experience of becoming a pastor. Resources for the stage *before* becoming a pastor's wife – the stage of *preparing* for that role – were non-existent, regardless of denomination.

Maybe that's because, as you'll see over and over in the following pages, there is no one way for a family to *do* seminary. To be sure, the Seminaries themselves are still trying to figure out how best to accommodate women and children into an institution that has for so many years been driven by and for men.

"Wives need to feel like they are part of the formation process," said Dr. Tim Saleska, the Dean of Ministerial Formation and Professor of Exegetical Studies at Concordia Seminary in St. Louis. Only in the past fifteen years or so has the seminary in St. Louis taken a hard look at the family's involvement in that formation process. But a 1986 report from the Committee on Creativity and Continuity says that the four-year M-Div program "tests a man and his family on practically every imaginable level."

I knew I couldn't write a road map that I had so craved. But perhaps there were some common denominators in the stories of

---

[4] For example, *Sacred Privilege: Your Life and Ministry as a Pastor's Wife*, by Kay Warren (wife of Saddleback Church Pastor Rick Warren) was published in 2017 (Revell), with a non-denominational Christian focus. *The Pastor's Wife: Strengthened by Grace for a Life of Love*, by Redeemer Church of Dubai pastor's wife Gloria Furman, was published in 2015 (Crossway). *You Can Still Wear Cute Shoes: And Other Great Advice from an Unlikely Preacher's Wife*, by Baptist pastor's wife Lisa McKay, was published in 2010 (David C. Cook).

women who were at the seminary with their husbands or freshly out of the seminary culture and in a new role of "pastor's wife." Perhaps through stories, which included candid advice, struggles and perseverance, joys and failures, we could launch a much-needed dialogue not only on the seminary campuses, but across the LCMS community at large. What have women left behind to faithfully follow their husbands/fiancés in their pursuit of public ministry? What have they gained? What did they risk? Where have they encountered moments of affirmation, and where have they had to summon all of their strength just to get through a moment?

How do women prepare to become pastors' wives?

I started to ask around. Would these women across two campuses with astonishingly diverse interests, ideas, backgrounds and vocations share their stories?

More than fifty women jumped at the chance, eager to contribute to the conversation about what common experiences unite us in our journeys of becoming pastors' wives.

As women, we are tossed into roles we never imagined having while our husbands pursue their theological education. It's phenomenal to me how God works in wildly different ways in different families and individuals. So much goes into the whole picture of the seminary experience. No adventure is unheard of.

"I wish I would have realized more that everyone's experience is a little bit different, and that you can make the most of it, if you want to," said Sherry Bolosan.

As diverse as we are, my conversations with women for this book showed me over and over again that the families at the seminary have a few things in common: No one knows what the future holds; no one knows how they will get from the present to whatever comes next; and every family at the seminary is pursuing an act of blind faith. Seminary asks us in big ways to release control and rely completely on God in situations that seem difficult or even impossible to navigate.

Most of us know that tried-and-true Bible verse: "Your word is a lamp for my feet, a light on my path" (Psalm 119:105). Have you ever visualized those words in action?

If you shine a lamp on your feet, you can't see very far ahead.

But that is where faith – that faith that can move mountains – does its work. If you could see the entire path stretched before you – if all the answers were lit up before you – would you keep walking? If you didn't have to trust God, would you keep going?

This book does not profess to have all the answers, and that's a good thing. Because God is the only One who sees it all. Yet I hope as you read you'll encounter a deep sense of hope in and excitement for the role that stretches unseen before you. So much goes into this wild journey of preparing to become a pastor's wife. I hope that the stories of the women in this book will resonate with you, and that perhaps you may even recognize yourself in some of them.

How do these stories collectively become *our story* of what God asks of us as women while He calls our men to seminary and then to serve a church body?

"In everything we do here, we have to have an open hand," said Kara Johnson.

Let me begin with this: If you are a woman who may or will be at the seminary soon, trust that God will give you strength when and where you need it. If you are a wife at the seminary right now, know that your struggles, your questions and your excitement are unique – but you are not alone. If you are a fiancé of a seminary student, be prepared for some tough choices ahead – and let God lead. If you are a new pastor's wife, untangling the mystery of that role even as you settle into life in a new community, a new home, a new church, you are already a strong woman. If you are a parishioner, you can understand how God may have worked in your pastor's wife to get her to your congregation. Wherever you are on the journey to becoming a pastor's wife, God is right there with you. His grace is sufficient. He is working, even now.

PART 1

The Decision

CHAPTER 1

Wrestling with God through the Decision

"Are you thinking about becoming a pastor?" Sherry Bolosan asked her husband, Chad.

"No," he replied.

Chad, who grew up on the Hawaiian islands of Oahu and Kauai and was baptized at age thirty, worked as an accountant in Schaumburg, Illinois. He listened to podcasts and videos by Concordia Seminary professors whenever he could. Sherry worked as a director of Christian education (DCE) at a Lutheran church in Schaumburg, and one of her co-workers was adamant: one day, Chad would be a pastor.

"I was like, 'Not all boys who love Jesus are going to be pastors,'" Sherry said.

In New York, Kristin Bayer asked her husband, Tim, the same thing: "Do you want to become a pastor?"

He always said no. Yet it was normal for Tim, a physicist who provided defense contracting, to crack open Martin Luther's *Book of Concord* whenever he had a minute to spare.

As a teenager, Michael McGinley had converted to the LCMS

from the Christian Reformed Church. He had started filling out the application paperwork for seminary when he met his wife-to-be, Kelsi, a Catholic from West Des Moines, Iowa. As they contemplated marriage, Kelsi struggled with what that meant for Michael's possible future as a pastor. A church leader who was married? Was that even okay?

Resistance. Denial. Uncertainty. God works through our shortcomings. And He's been doing it for centuries.

In Exodus chapter 3, God appeared to Moses in a burning bush. Moses, a shepherd and a foreigner who was living in exile, hid his face. He was afraid. He couldn't make sense of what was happening in front of him. From the burning bush, God Himself spoke: "… now, go. I am sending you …"[5]

Moses would be the one to rescue his people, the Israelites, from the heavy oppression they had suffered for so long at the hand of the Egyptians.

Yet, even with God's direct orders, Moses wasn't solidly convinced.

"Who am I that I should go …?" he asked to the fire.[6]

The struggle was real. Fear. Doubt. Unworthiness. The absurdity that a voice from a burning bush was prompting him to save a nation was enough for Moses to second-guess everything: who he was, what he was doing, where he would go next.

Yet, God was working.

The Bible is full of stories of the work He calls His people to do, and it is full of stories of how those people respond. God sent apostles to spread the news about who Jesus is and to make disciples. When Jesus told the apostles Peter, Andrew, James, and John to follow Him, the four men dropped their nets and obeyed immediately (Matthew 4:18-22). But most every prophet of the Old Testament struggled and hesitated over God's calling before

---

[5] Exodus 3:10
[6] Exodus 3:11

responding in faith. Jacob literally wrestled with God (Genesis 32:22-32). God sent Moses to fulfill a big and definite purpose, and Moses dragged his feet. God sent prophets to communicate astonishing messages to entire nations. Many, like Isaiah, carried out those messages, but not without facing a whole lot of fear head-on. Jonah simply ran away.

Eventually, Amos prophesied that God would stop speaking to his people. God would become silent because Israel – that same nation He had so graciously delivered from the Egyptians through Moses – had hardened their hearts. They would not listen to God. That period of silence came to an end when the angel appeared to Mary in Luke. God would send His Son.

These days, God rarely speaks through prophecies or via angels He sends to earth. He never appeared to anyone from a burning bush before or since Moses. But He does speak.

In her Bible study, *The Mighty & The Mysterious*, author and pastor's wife Heidi Goehmann writes, "God *can* do the work of His kingdom out of thin air and burning bushes, but He almost always chooses to do His work through people ..."[7]

One of the most difficult things about how He speaks today is that often His voice is hard to recognize.

For years my husband, Bryan, struggled with knowing the voice of God. How could he discern when God was speaking to him, how God was leading him? Moses had a burning bush. Couldn't Bryan have a billboard? Paul was struck blind, and then scales fell from his eyes. Couldn't God strike Bryan over the head and say, "Hey! Listen up!"

Bryan craved a sign – *something* concrete to point him in the right direction (whatever that was). He talked to close friends and family members about his struggle and the pulsing question on his heart: Should he become a pastor?

---

[7] Heidi Goehmann, *The Mighty & The Mysterious: A Study of Colossians* (St. Louis: Concordia Publishing House, 2019), 29.

Over and over, people affirmed that desire. *Go,* said the DCE of the church we were attending in Overland Park, Kansas. *What are you waiting for?*

Go, said his close friends, who knew he did not love his career as an engineer and could easily picture him thriving in ministry.

Go, said his family. *It's about time.*

Finally we realized that God was indeed speaking. He wasn't providing a billboard or appearing in a burning bush. He was speaking through the people we loved and trusted most.

Almost every journey to the seminary is wrought with struggle and intense discernment. So much seems to stand in the way between the lives we have and the lives to which the Holy Spirit may be calling us.

Like Moses, we come up against doubt. Numerous people encouraged David Jander, a DCE in Texas, to consider seminary. David and his wife, Coreen, were in their forties, had three school-aged children and were part of a close-knit church family. They were debt-free. On the surface, seminary made little sense.

"The process of prayer and discussion was a confusing one because of the season of life we were in," Coreen said.

Like Jacob, we encounter restlessness. Josh Vogel worked a family farm and served as a trustee at his church in Michigan. But he felt that God was calling him to step into a greater leadership role. As he worked the farm day in and day out, he questioned whether God was pushing him in a new direction.

Like Jonah, we push and push against the Holy Spirit's nudges until we are so exhausted that the only way to regain our energy is to put our full trust in Him. Kevin Barron, a former Catholic who had been disillusioned with the church during his youth, told his girlfriend, Leslie, that she would never see him attending her church. But during a four-month tour to Afghanistan in 2010, he started asking big questions about faith and God. He knew something was missing from his life. Over the process of several years, Kevin harnessed his deep theological questions into a pursuit to become an LCMS pastor.

Part of the mystery of the Holy Spirit is that it can work through anything at any time. God calls people to ministry in all kinds of ways. He uses doubt. He uses fear. He uses defiance. He uses wrong turns. He uses conversations with and influences of others. He uses time.

Julian Lamie was set to study pharmacy until the day he registered for college classes. Suddenly, he realized pharmacy was not at all what he wanted to do. The idea of ministry, which had always been in the back of his mind, roared to life.

But why then, at that moment?

"It took the reality of going down the wrong path to realize what he needed to be doing instead," said his wife, Juli.

Joe Nehring was eighteen months into Catholic seminary, preparing to become a priest, when he changed his mind because of a strong belief that God intended him to be a husband and a father. He found a job in the IT department at Boeing in St. Louis, married, and had two children with his wife, Linda. He worked at Boeing for thirty-one years, before he was laid off. That's when he decided to begin his theological training at Concordia Seminary, at age fifty-six.

Adam Bridgman graduated on the pre-seminary track at Concordia College-Mequon and attended Concordia Seminary in St. Louis for one year before deciding seminary was not for him. That was twenty years ago. He found work as a medical coding and billing auditor in his Illinois hometown, and returned to seminary two decades later.

God never stopped working on these men. He allowed Julian an error of judgment to further reinforce His actual plan. By realizing what he *didn't* want, Julian more clearly realized what he *did* want. God wasn't saying "no" to Joe Nehring or Adam Bridgman; He was just saying, "Not yet." He had other work for them to do first.

Part of the mystery of the Holy Spirit is that it can work through anything. Rarely is the path to serving Him easy or straightforward.

Yet, "How do you say no if God puts it on your heart?" asked Fadia Jenkins. Her husband, Jeff, walked away from a tenured career in architecture to pursue seminary – but only after challenging God that he would have to stop loving architecture before he considered a career in the ministry. In time, God answered that prayer: mounting frustrations over increased regulations and the eventual collapse of the housing market led Jeff to seek a new direction, years after God had initially put it on his heart.

Discerning God's timing when we feel led to a new endeavor is rarely easy. Often, it is downright confusing. How receptive are we to the transformative work of Christ in our lives? What are we willing to risk? What are we willing to leave behind?

Matt and Michelle Knauss drove nearly two thousand miles from their home in southern California to St. Louis, with their three kids – ages two, seven, and nine, in tow. They had no money saved for this new endeavor, and they knew that such a sudden, dramatic life change was downright crazy.

Yet they knew the Holy Spirit was at work. Like many others, Matt had resisted the call at first. He was a chef and restaurant manager who often went surfing with his pastor. From the surfboard one day, the pastor told Matt that the church needed strong men like Matt to shepherd congregations. Even though Matt initially said no, he and his family were headed to seminary less than a year later.

As I struggled with my own lack of desire to do this entirely new thing – pack up a life, move a family of four including two young children to another state for another temporary time span – I knew that struggle didn't hold a candle to what God had in store. God did not put seminary on my heart; He put seminary on my husband's heart. Who was I to question that?

I would not have chosen this particular point in our lives as the time for our family to go to seminary. But for some reason, God did. Even though it didn't make sense to me, I knew I would not argue with His grand plan.

Faith is often taking small steps forward, even if you can't see where you're going. God was providing enough light so that we could see directly in front of us – and no more.

In effect, He was saying, *Trust me.*

"God is faithful even when we take small steps in the dark," said pastor's wife Jenny Price.

Take a step forward and see if God blesses it.

As David and Coreen Jander prayed about the possibility of seminary, they both encountered an unlikely peace, even though neither of them could conceive of how they would pay for it or how they would pull up the roots they had put down in Texas. As they moved forward little by little, God continued to bless them, and their trust in God's plans and His timing became more and more solid.

Once Chad Bolosan realized that God might be prompting him to become a pastor, he and his family attended Next Steps, a weekend at Concordia Seminary designed for men and their families who are considering seminary. There, they heard someone say how amazing it is that God leads people with so many different personalities to the same ministry.

"I could just feel this release of tension," Sherry said. "And I was like, 'We're coming.'"

CHAPTER 2

Community in the Decision

Once a family has made the decision to go to seminary, life starts to change. I remember this burst of excitement that came with the finality of our decision. Suddenly my head was exploding with new ideas and questions: Where would we live in this new city? What sorts of opportunities would we encounter? Who would we meet? Where would our oldest child start Kindergarten? Could I continue doing the work I was already doing, or would I have to completely shift course?

What would our life look like?

Of course, beneath that energy and excitement is a perplexing brew of other emotions: anxiety, fear, confusion, apprehension, perhaps even sadness.

These emotions come up because a move to seminary requires that we give something up.

"I was expecting that we would be going into the wilderness," said Melissa Zech. Melissa and her husband, Rako, left a custom-built 2,400-square-foot home and moved with their six children from a Pennsylvania farm to a nine-hundred-square-foot apartment on the Concordia Seminary campus. *Wilderness* was about the perfect word.

When my husband and I decided that he should pursue seminary, we first thought we would go as soon as possible. Why wait if we knew this was the next step for our family?

But we quickly learned that we had to figure out some other dynamics first. How, for example, would Bryan go about quitting his work as an engineer, and how would he break that news to his co-workers and, most importantly, his boss? Walking away from a comfortable paycheck was big enough, but with Bryan's job we would also be leaving behind excellent health insurance. How would we be covered while he was in seminary? Concordia Health Plans offered a great health care package for seminary students and their families, but it was expensive. The other option was for me to find a job that offered health insurance. Was I really ready to give up being a stay-at-home mom, if our financial decisions came to that?

Even if the prompting to pursue a career in ministry is strong and undeniably from the Holy Spirit, the realities of life often stand in the way of a family making the leap to seminary right away.

As Sam and Kelsey Fink weighed their options in a Michigan hotel room on their way back home from their initial visit to Concordia Seminary, they knew there was a lot to think about. They were happily settled in a house they owned, in a neighborhood they loved. They ate dinner with friends in their neighborhood at least twice a week.

"We had a great life," Kelsey said. "We had the thing that people dream of."

Often, the thought of uprooting a family in the middle of a humming, stable life, keeps seminary at a distance. A major move often means a departure from a solid and familiar support system.

Chris and Liz Garcia and their young children would have to downsize in a big way, leaving a home they owned and loved in Michigan. Living on campus would be the most cost-effective option for them,[8] and that meant they would be occupying a space they could never really call their own. But the hardest part of the decision for Liz was moving away from her own family – her parents and her siblings – just as her daughters, ages two and three, were getting to know them. Regular, everyday interactions with those family members would no longer be possible, and family holidays and traditions would probably look a lot different, too.

In Pennsylvania, Rako and Melissa Zech lived a half mile from Melissa's parents, and intended to help take care of her parents as they aged. That is still an unsettling detail of seminary for Melissa.

"I feel like I shouldn't be leaving my family," she said, "like that's for bad people."

What we leave behind to come to seminary is no small order. There is so much to consider, from so many angles. Finances. Vocation. Housing. Family. Friends and neighbors. How do you move forward in joy when you're letting go of so much?

I wish I could tell you that it's easy once you make the leap to seminary. I wish I could say that you would look back at everything you felt like you gave up and realized that leaving it was no big deal. But I would be lying if I told you that. Committing to seminary and a life in ministry is hard. God tests our faith through this time. He will likely ask you to give up a lot. He challenges us to leave our comfort zones, take risks, and depend on Him.

And if you or your family waits until your life is in perfect order before you make the leap to seminary, you'll never go.

"Seminary can be something that you keep putting off," said Kelsey Fink. "It never makes sense to quit your job, sell your house … You have a million questions."

At some point, sacrifices and all, you just have to jump.

In their book, *The Pastor's Family: Shepherding Your Family*

---

[8] Concordia Seminary in St. Louis offers married student housing on campus in the form of two-, three- and four-bedroom apartments as well as townhomes. Concordia Theological Seminary in Fort Wayne has no on-campus married student housing.

through the Challenges of Pastoral Ministry, Pastor Brian and Cara Croft write, "If you are called and gifted for ministry, you must not avoid the pursuit of your call in the name of saving your family from the challenges of ministry."[9]

We can either choose to play it safe, risk nothing for our family, and hope for a happy and undisturbed life, or we can risk everything for God's kingdom and trust Him to carry us through. If God is calling and you play it safe, He will keep knocking and you will keep wondering, "What if ..." You will not grow in faith, and you will never be at peace.

During our time at the seminary, I came across this passage in an issue of *Today's Light*, a devotional published by Concordia Publishing House:

"It is far better for us to seek God's purpose for our lives rather than His plan ... the specific circumstances of life matter far less than God's will for our transformation into the image of His son."[10]

"Purpose" is the big picture, the ten-thousand-foot view. "Plan" is the series of smaller pictures, ten-foot views, that help us to achieve God's purpose. Rather than getting hung up in the smaller details of our circumstances, we should be asking how God might want to use us for His glory.

The *Today's Light* passage continues: "In tough decisions, ask: How can I, in this situation, reflect Jesus' wisdom, compassion, anger at sin, His forgiving grace toward sinners?

"These questions matter most in life. The rest are merely details. We can, in Christian freedom, make choices as we like, without fear."

Moving can be exciting. Transition can be exciting. You are invited, in a transition, to experience a new place. You are invited

---

[9] Brian Croft and Cara Croft, *The Pastor's Family: Shepherding Your Family through the Challenges of Pastoral Ministry* (Zondervan, 2013), 15.

[10] Jane Fryar, *Today's Light* (St. Louis: Concordia Publishing House, 2016), vol. 21 issue 4, Dec 7.

to meet new people – and learn more about yourself in the process. You face new experiences, new opportunities, and new ways of looking at the world and your place in it.

But life on the edge of that transition is often a murky place. How will the world around you respond to your leap of faith? How will your relationships – with friends, with neighbors, with family – be different? How will your own family be transformed?

Hebrews 11 tells us that the ancients – those prophets, disciples, and all-around regular people – were commended for their faith. They stepped forward, even though they could not clearly see what God was doing. Noah. Abraham. Sarah. Rahab. Abraham was called to go to a place and he went, even though he did not know where he was going. By faith, he made his home "like a stranger in a foreign country …"[11]

These ancients, in trust and godly fear, gave up what was familiar to them to enter a new space – a foreign country, a new role, a new way of thinking.

None of them would have taken that first step without faith in God who knew more than they did. None of them would have had the courage to act without the faith that the Holy Spirit placed in them. Faith, raw and pulsing, emboldened them to move forward in confidence, even when fear and uncertainty threatened to take back the reins.

Let Hebrews 11:1 anchor you on the edge of tremendous transition: "Faith is confidence in what we hope for and assurance about what we do not see."

God gives us the light we need, when we need it. If He gave us more, we would find less need to trust Him.

Leaving a comfort zone is almost always scary. But don't let fear cloud the truth that God promises to never leave you or forsake you. Don't let fear govern your faithfulness. Always choose faith over fear.

---

[11] Hebrews 11:9

CHAPTER 3

Contentment and Sacrifice in the Decision

> "Have I not commanded you? Be strong and courageous. Do not be afraid; do not be discouraged, for the Lord your God will be with you wherever you go."
>
> -Joshua 1:9

Even as he stood on a hill overlooking the valley of Canaan, Moses knew he would never cross the Jordan River and experience that "land of milk and honey" on the other side. He had doubted God (Numbers 20) and God's leading. Plenty of Israelites grumbled and moaned through God's direction. But Joshua, who, with Caleb had demonstrated unequivocal confidence that his people could defeat the powerful populations and their fortified cities scattered across the valley, was fired up. Moses spoke these words to Joshua in the presence of the whole Israelite nation: "The Lord himself goes before you and will be with you; he will never leave you nor forsake you. Do not be afraid; do not be discouraged" (Deuteronomy 31:8).

That promise that Moses gave to the Israelites thousands of

years ago stands just as true for us today. *He will never leave you nor forsake you.*

Nevertheless, many of us are like those Israelites today. We grumble and complain when God nudges us in a direction we don't necessarily like or totally agree with. We ask why we can't just stay in the status quo, or bask in our comfort zones. *Why* should we ever turn our backs on comfort, stability, even a sense of permanence – all seemingly good things – to leap into the unknown?

Life is a string of transitions. As people, we experience change in staggering doses. Moves. Roles. Life events.

Throughout my many life transitions – leaving home for college, marriage, career, having kids, moving and moving again – I have come to see a consistent message in my faith life: *don't grow too comfortable.* I have come to almost fear contentment, because usually contentment means that God is about to pull the rug out from under me. *Don't grow too comfortable,* He says, *because I have work for you to do.* If we hang out in a comfort zone for too long, we risk being idle, dead to the works God has in store for us. We risk losing enthusiasm and seeing opportunities in the every-day.

Perhaps you've heard the phrase, "God does not call the equipped. He equips the called." Moses is our classic example of this. He resisted God's prompting with practically every excuse and fear he could drum up.

"Who am I that I should go?" he asked God in the burning bush (Exodus 3:11).

God reassured him.

What if his people didn't believe that God was working through him? What if his people didn't listen to him?

God assured him, "I will be with you."

Moses lacked the ability to speak eloquently.

God told Moses He would appoint his brother, Aaron, as the public speaker.

Finally, with no firing power left, Moses simply said: "Please send someone else" (Exodus 4:13).

But God had work for Moses to do. He was calling Moses, and no one else. He would not let Moses off the hook.

When I asked women on both seminary campuses if their husbands had resisted the call to ministry at first, the responses were overwhelmingly *YES*.

Why? Well, for a lot of reasons. Many men, despite being encouraged by pastors, friends, family members or co-workers, felt that they were not equipped to become pastors themselves. Not good enough. Not smart enough. Not financially prepared enough. Content in their roles as breadwinners. Established in other careers.

Sam Fink was a salesman for an automotive engineering company in Michigan when his pastor asked him to meet with a seminary recruiter who would be visiting the church. Sam had never considered a career in pastoral ministry.

"Worst case scenario, you get a free dinner," their pastor said.

Sam and his wife, Kelsey, agreed to meet with the recruiter, Bill Wrede. When Wrede asked how interested Sam was in becoming a pastor on a scale of one-to-ten, with ten being the most interested, Kelsey answered six. Sam answered one.

Kelsey urged Sam to pray about a possible career in ministry. She knew her husband had what it took to be a church leader, and it was no secret the church needed pastors. Sam agreed to pray about it, even though he was not seeking a major life change.

Timothy Magill had dreamed of becoming a pastor when he was a boy. But he could not afford to attend college, let alone seminary. So he did his best to squelch his dream, figuring God was not leading him into ministry. He worked at McDonald's, sold computers for Sears, and eventually worked his way up in a technology firm, becoming a computer programmer. He was earning a six-figure income in northern California, commuting ninety minutes one way to his job, and he was miserable. When the economy downturned in 2009, three-quarters of his company were laid off, including him. Timothy and his wife, Mary, moved in with Mary's mom in New Mexico and poured their entire life savings and retirement into opening a restaurant. But even that was not the answer.

It seemed that, no matter where they turned, God was closing doors.

"God had to lay him off from a good job and close every possible door he tried to open for three years," said Mary.

It seemed as though God used a series of "*no's*" to point the Magills to His "*yes*" for them. By allowing them to experience frustration and defeat, He was reinforcing His will for Timothy. He had put the desire to be a pastor on Timothy's heart for a reason. Encouragement from pastors and four more years of hard discernment finally brought the Magill family to Concordia Theological Seminary. Timothy was fifty-three when he graduated from the M-Div program in 2020.

My husband resisted his call to ministry for a long time. There was nothing surprising about his fears. Some of those fears were about the seminary process itself, and some of his fears were about the life in ministry that followed. Going to seminary would mean giving up security for his family. He would be walking away from a healthy salary to return to school full time. He would be giving up the role of breadwinner for a time, and that meant I might no longer be able to stay at home with our kids.

And there was more. By going down this road, he would be asking his family to uproot and completely change their way of life. He worried about how his role as a pastor might influence his children's identities among their peers. What perceived stigmas and expectations would come with being a pastor's kid? Moreover, he wanted to protect his children from seeing the church as greedy or demanding because it requires too much of Dad's time. In short, he questioned whether his becoming a pastor would jeopardize his children's faith lives.

There was a lot at stake in making this leap.

As people, we crave stability – and yes, even predictability. That's what the Israelites wanted, too. At least back in Egypt, they would have had food and drink every day.

With stability also comes the sense of control.

"I knew that seminary meant moving four times in four years and being willing to go where you were sent," said pastor's wife Liz Garcia. "That takes a lot of trust in God's plan and a lot of letting go of what control I thought I had over my life."

But often, God has something better for us. He knows what is best for us, far beyond what we know. He certainly had something better for the Israelites, but He wasn't about to just hand it over. He wanted the Israelites – those imperfect people – to realize they could trust Him.

People give up many things to come to seminary. Both men and women walk away from established careers. Jim and Kim Bartok sold their martial arts business. Josh and Pam Vogel walked away from the family farm, where they had long assumed they would spend their lives. Beth Jones knew she would have to leave her high-powered job as a human resources director if her family came to seminary. Josh Hileman would have to leave a stable career in the military.

One of the most difficult hurdles for people to overcome as they are considering a transition into pastoral ministry is finances. Financial stability takes on different forms: a steady job, a reliable paycheck, even the comfort of living close to family, where you may have built-in babysitters and an occasional free meal. The thought of letting go of that financial stability is enough to scare families into thinking twice about making the leap into ministry.

Questions abound: How much does a seminary education cost? What sort of financial aid is available? What will our financial situation look like on the other side, when we are serving in a church? What sacrifices will be necessary to make this new life work?

"We were so unsure if seminary was even possible," said Michelle Knauss. "No one ever really told us how much it was going to cost."

Beth Meier echoed that uncertainty.

"My only question [about seminary] was how people survived," she said. "It didn't seem possible without getting $100,000 in debt."

Considering the financial impact of seminary is not a clear-cut process. So many factors go into analyzing what a family budget will look like during those four years and what a seminary education will cost in the long run.

Anna Davis remembers the tired frustration that crept over her every time she heard the answer to how seminary works financially: *It just does. The Lord provides.*

"I hated that answer," Anna said. "I wanted to know the bottom line."

Melissa Zech resigned herself to the probability that her family would be eating "just enough." With 6 kids, the family went through two loaves of bread a day. Even without seminary in the picture, it was a very expensive time in their lives.

Before we made the move to seminary, my husband and I outlined a mock budget, postulating how his pursuit of this four-year degree might impact our family financially. We factored in all of the basics – a house payment, utilities, groceries, car insurance, etc. We analyzed a budget with my meager freelance income, and we analyzed a budget with a conservative estimate of a salary I could bring in should I return to full-time work outside of the home. But we also had to factor in the cost of the education itself. Thankfully, the seminary offers many scholarship opportunities that cover a wide range of demographics, circumstances, and family dynamics. We looked at every scholarship the seminary listed, and we applied for each one that somehow fit our situation.

We also knew that many congregations and individuals

graciously supported Seminarians, through the seminary's Adopt-a-Student program and private donations. The seminary assured us that we would receive Adopt-A-Student funds, but we had no idea what that looked like.

In the end, we worked with what we knew to build a plausible financial blueprint for seminary. We didn't have all of the answers, but we knew we had to trust that God would provide in the details we could not yet see.

Melissa Zech was shocked to realize that her family encountered fewer financial worries at the seminary than they did on their farm in Pennsylvania.

"The way that God provides has been amazing," Melissa said. "It's just new provisions and new ways of getting to know Him."

At the end of the day, trusting God to help you work out the financial piece of seminary is a wild act of faith. Together, you are trusting Jesus, and you are trusting in God's provision. You will find that needs get met in wildly different ways. You might recognize yourself in the story of the Israelites wandering the desert: "Okay, God. You led us here. Where's the food?" But then, it comes.

Proverbs 3:5-6 tells us: "Trust in the Lord with all your heart and lean not on your own understanding; in all

Four Ways to Prepare for Seminary

1. **Pray.** First Thessalonians 5:17 tells us to "pray without ceasing" (English Standard Version translation). Talk to God openly about your fears AND your excitements over seminary. Be honest; He knows everything that's on your mind already. When you pray, take time to listen. In the silent moments, where do you feel God speaking? Do you feel His resistance anywhere? Do you feel your heart quicken in nervous energy over the next steps? Look at the verses on either side of 1 Thessalonians 5:17. Chapter 5 verse 16 tells us to "Rejoice always." Chapter 5 verse 18 says to "give thanks in all circumstances for this is the will of God for you in Christ Jesus." So while we pray, we should also rejoice and give thanks. Thank God that He has placed the desire for pastoral training on your husband's heart. Then, ask for His guidance and strength to lead you one step at a time on the journey.

2. **Move in with a relative.** A year before they came to the seminary, the Erica and Nate McCarty moved in with Erica's aunt in another big push to save money. Nate took ad hoc Greek lessons from their pastor and worked at the church to gain ministry

experience. When it came time to move to seminary, the McCartys had a sizeable nest egg saved. They were already somewhat transitory, so completely uprooting was not a huge deal. This type of planning took incredible foresight and a willingness to be less settled for a time. For the McCartys, it was totally worth it.

3. **Apply for scholarships, as a team.** Apply for scholarships. This is essential, and there's a good chance that in searching you'll find more financial aid than you anticipated. It is possible to get out of seminary without taking on debt. But most scholarships don't just show up on your doorstep. You and your husband must do the work to make them real.

Help your husband find and apply for scholarships. As we prepared to move to St. Louis, Bryan and I made a list of scholarship opportunities we wanted to pursue. We started with the list here: https://www.csl.edu/admissions/financial-aid/scholarships/all-scholarships/ I helped him by filling in the basics, such as name and address. That left only the open-ended questions up to him. By making the pursuit of scholarships a team effort, we were able to divide and

your ways acknowledge him and he will make your paths straight."

Part of listening and watching for the Holy Spirit to move is paying attention and always being open to what God has in store, even if what He hands you isn't at all what you expected. God is so much bigger than our basic needs! If He moves your family toward formal pastoral ministry, He will work out every detail for His glory. If the thought of leaving a comfort zone makes you want to crawl into the floor, know that God is working, even through your reluctance. If you have been waiting for your husband to *finally* see that seminary is the way to go, know that God is working in the desire of your heart.

John 14:15 shows us the direct relationship between love and obedience. Jesus tells His disciples, "If you love me, keep my commands." Love for our guiding Father goes hand-in-hand with our obedience to Him; we cannot love God and at the same time ignore His prompting.

As you think about what the pursuit of a pastoral career means for your family, know that God will ask a lot of you. He might ask you for more than you think you or your family can handle. But if He has called you to seminary, He won't leave you hanging.

He reassures us, even as He reassured His disciples: "Peace I leave with you; my peace I give you. I do not give to you as the world gives. Do not let your hearts be troubled and do not be afraid."[12]

The journey into pastoral ministry is largely a journey that challenges our notions of contentment. What is contentment and how can we rest in it? We'll talk more about this in future chapters, but when it comes down to it, being content is knowing that things will happen in God's time, not yours, and to rest (not worry) in that.

"Seminary for us was a process of refinement," said Jenny Price.

The process of moving makes you evaluate your possessions, your roles, your relationships, over and over again. Oftentimes, that evaluation process can be a celebration or a sort of passage from one point in life to the next.

Transition is not simply a fact of life. It is God's way of reminding us over and over again to trust Him. Not only is transition a *part* of life; it is *most* of life.

At its base, *transition* is simply *movement*. As a writer, I learned pretty quickly that a story needs conflict to

conquer, and our financial aid was beyond sufficient.

4. **Minimize**. As they prepared to move to seminary, David and Coreen Jander thought about what life might look like for a missionary family. Of course they weren't missionaries in the traditional sense; they were moving from one state to another so that David could pursue a four-year Master's degree. But a general life rule of missionaries – *live with less* – still made a lot of sense. They sold most of their furniture and household items. Coreen became comfortable asking people if they had hand-me-downs for her three children.

"People love to be generous and share clothes with someone they know instead of dropping off [unwanted clothes] at a thrift store," she said. "These were big lifestyle shifts for us and they made a huge different in our ability to avoid debt."

---

[12] John 14:27

capture a reader's attention. That has always been funny to me, because I don't *like* conflict. Who does?

But if you think about it, conflict, like transition, is simply movement in a story. If you don't have movement – ups and downs – you have stagnation. On a heart rate monitor, ups and downs are critical: they point to life. A flat line means death.

We can't have ups if we don't have downs. We can't know triumph if we haven't experienced defeat. We can't know confidence if we don't also know insecurity. We can't live in the light without understanding what it's like to be in the dark.

"Ministry is hard," writes Brian Croft.[13] "Sacrifice is *always* necessary."

---

[13] Croft, *The Pastor's Family: Shepherding Your Family Through the Challenges of Pastoral Ministry*, 15.

CHAPTER 4

Faith in Your Role in the Decision

One of the biggest questions women face as they consider with their husbands a possible leap to seminary is: *Who am I in this process?*

How will you continue to live out your own vocation as a wife, a mother, a working professional or any combination of those roles, while your husband is fulfilling his own calling? How will your role at seminary be different than your role prior to seminary?

Shortly before Latashia Lynne Roll moved with her family to Concordia Seminary from Colorado Springs, she courageously posted this message on the Women of Concordia Seminary Facebook page:

Hi ladies! God is allowing me to experience a phase in my life where I know nothing, have no answers, and need to put my full trust in Him. While I'm thankful for this growth period, I also need to be proactively seeking where He may provide. I am currently a stay at home mom. I nanny to help with the bills. I would love to be able to do something similar while we are at seminary, as I understand that my husband will have plenty of demands on him for school ... If any of you know of any job that I could do while I have my little girl with me, please keep me informed! I've had some interviews, yet all have fallen through.

This message is a neatly packaged version of what so many women coming to the seminary experience. According to Celina Haupt, who served a new role at Concordia Seminary as Women's Coordinator from 2014-2019, identity is the number-one struggle women at seminary face. It's difficult to address that struggle concretely, because the question of *Who am I in all of this?* looks different for everyone. A map for life as a pastor's wife can look a thousand different ways.

When our husbands accept God's vocational prompting to go to school to become a pastor, we as women are also preparing to take on a new role, whether we want to or not. If your husband becomes a pastor, you, by default, assume the role of pastor's wife.

It's probably no surprise that not every woman is initially excited at the thought of her husband attending seminary. In fact, many women cringe at the thought, feeling unworthy or opposed to living up to the perceived high expectations of a pastor's wife.

Liz Garcia said that God worked on her heart in a major way in the years leading up to her family's journey to seminary.

"I did NOT want to go to seminary or be a pastor's wife," said Liz.

Liz knew several pastors' wives, all with different talents and personalities. All of them appeared to be so involved in church, energetic, and extroverted. It seemed to Liz that being a pastor's wife required this sort of constant energy and willingness to be in the spotlight. Yet Liz had always been more of a behind-the-scenes person. She hated the thought of being the center of attention. She imagined how the lives of these pastors' wives were constantly on display. It was not a life Liz thought she wanted.

"I began to pray earnestly for God to soften my heart," Liz said.

Leslie Barron was struck with a momentary fear when her husband, Kevin, announced he was ready to take the step to seminary. She was not pastor's wife material. She thought, "Oh, no! I know my husband was meant for this. I know he was built for this. But I'm going to mess it up for him!"

Leslie encountered the same sort of fear Liz did, but in a different way. She imagined that her life would be on display as a somewhat unruly extrovert who was full of sin. She cursed sometimes. She practiced Jujitsu. She was a government contractor with top-secret security clearance.

What is it about the term "pastor's wife" that causes so much angst? When my husband was an engineer, I did not think of myself as an engineer's wife. I don't know of any women who define themselves as the teacher's wife or the contractor's wife. Why is becoming a pastor's wife such a big deal?

Even before we came to seminary, I could think of few other roles that carried with them such a burden of stereotypes. Society does not harbor stereotypes for an engineer's wife or a contractor's wife. Yet we all know the common perception of the pastor's wife.

Erica McCarty, whose husband is Pastor at Bethlehem Lutheran Church in Jacksonville Beach, Florida, described the cookie cutter mold of a pastor's wife this way: "A pastor's wife is [stereotypically] spiritually all put together, in the Word, out doing things for others, extroverted."

On top of that, she probably plays the organ, leads Sunday school, directs the VBS program, and always shows kindness and patience to others. She never puts herself first.

But my conversations with women at the seminary paint a different picture of today's "pastor's wife." More than half of us consider ourselves introverts, not extroverts. Many women I spoke with expressed insecurities over *not* being spiritually all put together.

I think the common stereotypes of the pastor's wife is just one more way Satan gains a foothold to convincing us we don't have what it takes to fulfill a God-given role. Sin's grip on the world means that we often struggle with feeling like we're *enough*. We have high expectations of ourselves as wives, mothers, daughters. For the outside world to place additional expectations on us – expectations that are not attached to just anyone – we can easily feel defeated before we ever get started. As women, who by nature already wrestle in every area of their life with not being *enough,* it's a tall order to have yet one more expectation placed on you – to be *extroverted/moral/self-controlled/fill-in-the-blank* enough to be a pastor's wife.

We wrestle with that thought so much because it's true: we are *not* enough.

But here is another truth: Satan loves to interfere with our responses to God's will in any way he can. He helps us to believe and zero in on how we're not "enough" by helping us forget the significance of Christ's death on the cross – and the freedom we have in Christ because of it.

"Satan wants our thoughts totally focused on the fleshly concerns, our emotions conflicted and confused, our wills weakened by indecision and preoccupation with self," writes Joanna Weaver.[14]

As my family prepared to make the leap to seminary, I knew I would likely have to put some of my own ambitions on hold. I had worked through a lot of doubts, insecurities, and transitions to finally achieve what I thought was a nearly ideal work-life balance. It had taken years, but finally, I was learning how to blend my freelance writing, editing, and teaching with my roles of wife and mom.

Seminary, I knew, would change all of that. I knew I might have

---

[14] Joanna Weaver, *Having a Mary Spirit: Allowing God to Change Us from the Inside Out* (Waterbrook Multnomah, 2006), 111.

to go to work full-time, something I had not done since before we had kids. The mock budgets we had worked through made it clear that we could not depend on my meager income as a freelance writer to get us through seminary. But putting my writing on hold scared me. I had finally felt like my writing career was beginning to take off. Was I really going to set that aside, after I'd worked at it for so long? Moreover, if I returned to work full time, I would not be as available and flexible for our boys. After years of growing into the stay-at-home parent role, fighting it, and crying over it and feeling like I was just not made for it, I had found my niche. As my boys grew and learned about the world, I was right there, learning with them. I didn't miss a moment. What would I miss – what moments would pass me by – if I worked full-time?

Ashley Brandmahl remembers the shift in thinking behind her husband's decision to pursue seminary. Both she and her husband, Josh, had planned to be teachers. Now, he was going into the ministry instead. How much would her job as a teacher factor into his Call?

Thinking about the nature of your role through the seminary years is one thing. But it's also crucial to consider what your role will look like after

Health Insurance
The Concordia Plan or Something Else?

One of the biggest factors to consider when coming to seminary is where you'll get health insurance. Both seminaries offer health insurance through the Concordia Health Plan (CHP), and both seminaries strongly encourage students to enroll in the seminary's health plan, unless granted a waiver. In St. Louis, the waiver must list proof of equivalent insurance coverage elsewhere. In Fort Wayne, it must include "eligible opt-outs," or legitimate reasons why one is denying participation in the CHP. Eligible opt-outs include health coverage under a spouse's or parent's health plan, coverage through military as a retiree, and other reasons, which are outlined on the Enrollment Form.

The seminaries pledge that their health plans are competitive and comprehensive. Many students and families defer to the CHP as part of a total seminary enrollment package.

But many other seminary families choose health insurance other than the CHP, because of the cost.

When my husband was at the seminary, we were surprised to learn that a monthly premium payment for CHP for our family would have rivaled our mortgage payment. While my employer did not offer health insurance as a benefit, it paid a stipend for health insurance through the Affordable Care Act. We found that our children qualified for state-sponsored health insurance due to our income. Overall, through our health insurance with the ACA, we paid about a quarter of what we would have paid through CHP. Our coverage through the ACA was not as comprehensive as it would have been had we gone with CHP, but because we were an overall healthy family with no ongoing medical issues, we decided a lower cost, less comprehensive plan was the best choice for our family during those four years.

The health insurance scene is changing all the time. So messy and complex, it is difficult to fully understand all of your options at any given time. Take the time to do your research and consider all options before deciding the best health insurance plan for your family. Don't be afraid to ask questions, and don't be afraid to start a dialogue with other seminary families about their approach to health insurance. You might even find that others have the same questions you do.

In the end, CHP might be the best choice for your family. But don't simply assume it is, without considering all of the options available to you.

The lesson here is: Do your homework.

For more information about the Concordia Health Plan for seminary students, visit https://www.concordiaplans.org/.

seminary, once your significant other is a pastor.

If I put my writing career on the back burner, would it suffer long-term?

Which call was higher, Josh Brandmahl's to be a pastor, or Ashley Brandmahl's to teach? Would it be possible for both of them to pursue their God-given vocations at the same time?

Is seminary worth risking all of this?

As women, it is fair to say we give up a lot when we faithfully follow our husbands to seminary. Some women transition from being a stay-at-home parent to a full-time working professional. Other women transition from being a full-time working professional to a stay-at-home parent. Still others leave a highly specialized job in their career field for a position that requires less specialized training or education.

The truth is, before coming to seminary, no one can see exactly what He is going to ask of us. He might ask in the immediate moment that we give up our home or our community or living in proximity to family. He might ask that we take our eyes off of a comfortable paycheck or put off a wife's career advancement. He might even ask that we take one step – and then another and another – in the dark, trusting that He is leading even if we can't see the way ahead.

Always, He is putting our faith to the test.

This verse from Paul was my cornerstone throughout seminary: "However, I consider my life worth nothing to me; my only aim is to finish the race and complete the task the Lord Jesus has given me—the task of testifying to the good news of God's grace" (Acts 20:24).

In the end, we simply have to trust that God knows what He's doing. Isaiah 55:8 reminds us, "For my thoughts are not your thoughts, neither are your ways my ways," declares the Lord.

God is not going to waste this experience. God is not in the business of wasting anything.

PART 2

Life At Seminary

CHAPTER 5

Wrestling with God at the Seminary

"The life of Mary shows that great things, important things, always begin with someone saying yes to God, and then moving along one yes at a time."

-Joanna Weaver, *Having a Mary Spirit*

Transition brings with it exhilaration and excitement. Everything is new. The possibilities are seemingly limitless. You view every-day moments and circumstances in a different light. You may find yourself re-examining or renewing goals, big and small.

Transition also brings with it overwhelm and chaos. Starting over can be terrifying. You fear the unknown. You long for a sense of order. So much seems out of your control.

The transition to seminary also brings with it a mountain of decisions. Where will you live? What will you do while your husband is in school full time? If you have school-aged children, where will they attend school? Priorities are different for each family.

When we moved to St. Louis, I remember thinking we were strangers in a strange place. Major decisions were facing us left and right. We bought a ninety-year-old brick home a mile south of campus. We hoped our decision to buy instead of rent would work out in our favor in the long run, but of course that wasn't a guarantee. Living near campus meant my husband's commute to school would be easy. But if I went to work, there was no guarantee I could find a suitable job close to campus and close to our house. Moreover, the home we bought was in a poor school district. That made us re-think our philosophies on private schooling. Even if we wanted to send our kids to private school, could we afford it?

And always, this question hung over the whole flurry of decisions: How would we know we were making good choices?

I had thought I was ready for this new start. My husband and I had endured countless long talks about what a move to seminary would look like. In theory, we knew the risks and the areas of our lives we would grieve by coming to St. Louis. We knew the likelihood of our decision paying off in the long run was high. We knew, despite the many challenges, that this move would probably be worth it. We knew God was watching over us, every step of the way.

So I was surprised at the ugly resentment that welled up in me during my husband's first year at the seminary. We were here, in a brand-new place, starting over with everything, because of *him*. All of these decisions that were coming at us were because of *him*. We left dear friends, a strong school for our boys, and a solid opportunity for me to build my writing career, because of *him*. We had traded one temporary place for another: just as Kansas City was not our permanent stop, St. Louis wouldn't be either. It didn't matter that I *wanted* to settle down. God wasn't allowing us that opportunity yet.

The temporary nature of our time at the seminary rubbed at me from all angles during our four years in St. Louis. It seemed that everywhere I turned, I was reminded how *not from here* I was. No, I didn't know where JJ Twiggs was, on Hampton across the street from the Dad-O. I didn't drive past Fuzzy's Tacos enough to know their Tuesday special, and I certainly didn't understand this city's penchant for gooey butter cake, a delectable I had never heard of.

It wasn't until after we moved to St. Louis and I talked to women about their own experiences that I realized self-pity was a common thorn, especially during the first year of seminary. We feel sorry for ourselves and what we are leaving behind to forge this path.

Erica McCarty admitted to falling into this mindset: *If I don't feel bad for me, who will?*

"The focus is very much on men, as it should be," she said, "but the wives are supposed to be quietly supportive in a variety of ways while maintaining the home. It felt like such an unrealistic expectation."

The move to seminary brought on more challenges than Chad and Sherry Bolosan anticipated. They would sell their home in the northwest Chicago suburb of Schaumburg and move to an apartment on the Concordia Seminary campus in St. Louis. They would shift from two incomes to one part-time income. Student loans were unavoidable.

Chad moved a week earlier than the rest of the family, to start summer Greek. That left Sherry with the majority of the packing and the final details of their home sale, all with three children underfoot.

The year prior to their move, Sherry had been excited and supportive.

"I had heard these great things about the seminary community," she said.

Moving didn't scare her. She simply saw it as the next step toward what God was calling her family to do.

But, with half of their stuff on the lawn outside their apartment on campus, Sherry fell apart. Here was her life – her family's

**The Seminary Wife's
Call to Church Work**

While the Lutheran Church-Missouri Synod only ordains men as pastors, many women pursue church work careers as Directors of Christian Education (DCEs) or deaconesses. Of the women I interviewed for this book, nearly one-fifth are trained (or are training to become) Directors of Christian Education (DCEs) or deaconesses within the LCMS. Both deaconesses and DCEs are certified, called and commissioned positions within the LCMS. As a result, it is difficult for couples in which the man is pursuing a pastoral career and the woman pursuing a career as a deaconess or DCE to simultaneously advance their vocational pursuits. Rarely will a trained deaconess or DCE receive a call to the same church or city where her husband is called as a pastor, primarily because neither the position nor the budget is there. In a report to the Board for National Mission in 2019, Deaconess Grace Rao, Director of LCMS Deaconess Ministry, said many churches would love to bring on trained deaconesses yet lack the money to hire another employee.

As a result of this complex mix of vocational calls and thin budgets, well over half of the women I spoke to who were pursuing careers as DCEs or deaconesses either put their own church worker career on hold or left it entirely when their husbands

life – in boxes on a lawn hundreds of miles from anywhere she knew.

"I suddenly didn't want to do this anymore," she said.

Resentment and self-pity are two common roadblocks that get in the way of our fully trusting God on the journey to seminary. But if we really think about it, roadblocks and distractions crop up at seemingly every turn along the transition. Satan will do whatever he can to thwart God's plan. Leslie Barron was thirty weeks pregnant when she and her husband, Kevin, moved to seminary from the Washington, D.C. area. Was *now* really the best time to go? she questioned. Numerous appliances quit working and a daughter broke her arm as Rako and Melissa Zech prepared to leave their Pennsylvania farm for seminary. Was God telling them not to do this? Michael and Kelsi McGinley had a new baby as they prepared to leave family and friends in Iowa for seminary. Did this make any sense?

At an Advent by Candlelight dinner at Ascension Lutheran Church in St. Louis during our second year at the seminary, speaker Jane Fryar zeroed in on Mary and her absolute trust in God. Luke 1 tells us that an angel visited Mary and told her she was going to give birth to a son. Mary was greatly troubled at first. She tried to discern what sort of greeting this might be. She questioned the angel's voice: How can this be possible? And the angel responded, "nothing will be impossible with God."[15]

Mary responded in faith: "I am the servant of the Lord; let it be to me according to your word."[16]

God directed every detail of Mary and Joseph's journey to Bethlehem. With a full-term pregnancy, it must have seemed to Mary like a terrible time to make the journey to Bethlehem. But Mary and Joseph were simply doing what they had to do.

I had read this story of Mary and the difficult journey to Bethlehem many times. But I had never meditated on how completely Mary had placed her life and the life of her family in God's hands. Absolute trust in God is so beautifully displayed in Mary's life. Why couldn't I trust God more with the details of our own lives and the temporary nature of this season?

As human beings, we long for comfort and peace. Scripture is filled with stories of people who hesitate when God tells them to go. Why? Because that's

went to seminary. The question, "How will my role as a church worker fit with my husband's call to a church, if at all?" echoed like a refrain through these interviews. By and large, these women recognize that God shapes and guides their vocations on more than a professional level. Their vocations as wives – and often as mothers – come first. That doesn't necessarily mean God is closing doors on a profession, though. He might just be saying, "Not yet," or, "Wait until you see what I have in store for you!"

Read on for snapshots of eight women with DCE or deaconess training whose husbands are in or are pursuing full-time ministry:

Leah Wendorff knew she might not ever be a DCE again once she met her husband-to-be, Aaron, because seminary was on his radar. If he pursued a seminary education, Leah knew he would eventually receive a call that would likely have little bearing on her DCE training.

But that possibility didn't bother her. More important than "DCE" was her role as a mother and the work of raising children. Leah remained optimistic through seminary that wherever her husband was ultimately called, she could use her God-given gifts and DCE training, even if in a strictly volunteer capacity.

"We've definitely looked at it as *our* ministry," Leah said.

---

[15] Luke 1:37 (ESV)
[16] Luke 1:38 (ESV)

Kyla Rodriguez found work as a DCE during the four years her husband, Adam, was enrolled in seminary. During Adam's first and fourth years of seminary, Kyla held the same seasonal position for the National Youth Gathering at the International Center in St. Louis. The position is special to the National Youth Gathering, and Kyla said the center loves to hire seminary wives for it.

Striking gold with her employment opportunities while at the seminary was a huge encouragement for Kyla, because she was continually being affirmed in what she loves to do.

Kyla said she believes God prepared her heart to be flexible in her desire for ministry.

"God has woven a job for me out of what seems like thin air most of the time," she said.

Krista Weeks was working on becoming a DCE when her then-boyfriend, Kyle, told her he wanted to become a pastor. Her first two years at Concordia University in Irvine, California, were stressful. Krista and Kyle were married, and she planned on doing the required internship for her DCE studies in St. Louis once they moved to the seminary. Yet, the further down the road of a DCE career she went, the less called she felt. She knew she and Kyle would have a difficult time ahead of them if she was a DCE and he was a pastor, because both of them would be called.

what we do as people. We doubt. We cling to comfort more than we cling to trust in God. We long to be in control, to know everything, to see the path before us.

Suzy Brakhage was filled with uncertainties as she and her husband left their beloved home in Oklahoma for seminary. They were leaving a house that they loved, and Suzy was walking away from a good job as a speech pathologist. She had no idea if she would be able to find similar work in St. Louis while her husband attended school. Yet even amidst the uncertainties, Suzy understood that they would be risking far more if they didn't go to seminary.

"I think we would have struggled with wondering if we were doing what God was calling us to if we'd stayed in Tulsa," she said.

If all we do is look back at where we came from and focus on what we know and what we can control, we cannot look with joy on where God is leading us. We can't place our trust in God if we don't step out *in faith*.

When Katie Schultz reflects on her and her husband's decision to come to seminary, she thinks about the life stage her family was in at that transition point. Soon they would have needed to put all three of their kids in daycare, which was not financially feasible. A fourth baby was on the way, and the home they lived in would have been too small for four kids.

"In some ways, it would have been harder to stay," Katie said.

God prepared the way for them to more easily come to the seminary as they were at a natural transition point in life.

A move to seminary actually meant a move closer to parents for Coreen Jander. During her husband's time at seminary, Coreen's mother was diagnosed with cancer. Because her family lived nearby, Coreen was able to be physically present with her mom through the cancer's most difficult stages. Moreover, she could celebrate with her mom in person upon her mom's successful completion of chemotherapy and return to good health.

"The Lord sees the big picture of our lives, and it amazes me to consider all the little details He knew needed to be fleshed out in this place," Coreen said.

Trace the Israelites' journey from Egypt to the Promised Land, and you'll see God reminding them over and over that He is their God and that He will take care of them.

Yet we can't avoid the truth that this vulnerable time of transition challenges all aspects of family. Regardless of who you are, your family dynamics will change when you make the move

What were the chances of them both being called to the same city?

Krista abandoned her pursuit of a DCE career after Kyle's first year at the seminary and found a job in childcare.

While Krista acknowledged this as a reality, it wasn't easy for her.

"I'm trying to figure out what I want to do," she said. "And I feel like I can't do that until we're out of seminary."

She admitted that during their years at seminary, she felt stuck.

"My jobs here are not my passion," she said. "I'm just trying to get us through school."

Even though she seemed to be at a fork in the road, Krista never lost faith that God was working. She knew God was asking her to wait on Him.

"I've just been trying to rest in, 'This is where God has me. There's a reason why I'm here and in this moment,'" she said.

Like Leah, Krista looks forward to belonging to a church her husband pastors and using her gifts there.

"I feel like seminary is very much a wilderness experience," she said. "We're all preparing for our Promise Land ... [But] God does amazing things in the wilderness, too. I'm trying to lean into that and just be patient."

As a DCE, Sherry Bolosan was called to St. Peters Lutheran Church in Schaumburg, Illionis, in 2004. But even then, she knew that God might call her into a different vocation or career further down the road. Now, she realizes the possibility is very real that she might not be able to be a church worker anymore. "I feel lost when it comes to that," she says. "Where is my purpose?"

During her husband's vicarage in Ohio, Sherry worked off and on with the youth of the congregation, but she found it was difficult to juggle her own role as a mother with ministry responsibilities. If both she and her husband were called church workers with Sunday-morning duties, she realized, she would need an extra support system for her own children on Sunday mornings.

"I still wonder what God has planned for me," Sherry said, "but I know that whatever it is, I will still be able to use my training as a DCE."

Erica McCarty was a trained DCE when she arrived at the seminary with her husband, Nate. But, with a five-year-old daughter, she had not worked as a DCE for several years. Erica had been her husband's biggest cheerleader on his road to ministry, and she was eager to support him however she could when they arrived in St. Louis.

"I'm like, whatever job you need me to do, I'll do it," she said.

For the first two years of seminary, she worked as a preschool assistant at a Lutheran school. She brought her daughter to seminary. A transition of this magnitude affects everyone involved in some way; no one is immune.

The seminaries work hard to provide tangible resources such as off-campus housing and job opportunities, school and childcare information, and community services, in concentrated efforts to help families with the complex relocation process. Lean into the resources that exist. Don't be afraid to ask questions. Don't be afraid to ask for help.

And don't be afraid to be vulnerable. Everyone on campus is in their own phase of transition. If we don't communicate our questions, then how can we ever hope to move a dialogue forward about the experience of becoming a pastor's wife? If we're not bold about sharing our insecurities, then how can we expect anyone else to be?

Juli Lamie felt a new sense of discord when she left her family in England to join her husband, Julian, in St. Louis. Her family understands and supports her living so far away from them. But the practical issues, such as calculating a six-hour time difference, constantly wore on her and them. Juli found that to maintain strong relationships with her parents and her sister, all of them had to be intentional in their connections.

"It's a skill you have to develop," she said.

One of the dynamics of family that Juli misses the most is the lack of spontaneity that comes with not living physically close to one another. No longer could she share many of her day-to-day moments with the people she loved most.

Juli's situation is an extreme example; few women leave their families on the other side of the world to join their husband at a seminary. But her story clearly illustrates some of the most common struggles that families at the seminary encounter: navigating different time zones, missing out on sharing with extended family the more trivial day-to-day moments, and the importance of being intentional in your interactions and communication.

But family dynamics change in positive ways, too. At first, Aaron and Leah Wendorff mourned the loss of free babysitting when they moved to seminary. The Wendorffs had lived fifteen minutes from Leah's parents prior to moving to Fort Wayne. But without family nearby, the Wendorffs saw that they were beginning to define their own identity as a family unit, apart from the extended family they were so accustomed to being around.

"Being away from family has helped us to just be us," Leah said.

with her. While Nate was on vicarage in Florida, Erica gave birth to twins. She has been a stay-at-home mom ever since.

Erica admitted that the transition from working professional to being solely a mom and a wife hasn't always been easy. Both husbands and wives wrestle with how to make their vocations work alongside each other's. At the seminary, Nate was a student. But he also worked as a gas station attendant to help pay the bills. That meant his roles as husband and father sometimes took a back seat. Meanwhile, Erica's roles as wife and mother were front and center.

"I'm realizing things aren't going to be the way I planned them, but that doesn't mean there can't be goodness in that, or peace," she said.

In this season, Erica said she is learning about and focusing more on who God has created her to be, and less on what she does.

As a deaconess student, Rachell Highley found herself navigating multiple communities at the seminary. She tried hard to connect with both her deaconess classmates and the wives of seminary students, because she is both. In their third year of seminary, Rachell wore yet more hats. She was a new mother, a deaconess intern, and a vicar's wife.

Looking to the future, Rachell admitted she didn't know how her call as a deaconess would fit with her husband's call as pastor. She knew her future as a deaconess may well not fit at all with her husband's career as pastor.

"My fear is not having a place in his call," she said. "Since I am also a called church worker it is quite possible that he will get a call and I will not."

Rachel Geraci grew up on the seminary campus at Fort Wayne, the daughter of a seminary professor. She was in her third year of deaconess training in St. Louis, on internship, when she met her husband, Coleman. In her deaconess classes, she had learned to think about the role of deaconess as a whole identity – not simply a label.

"God was pulling me in every direction into what I am today," she said.

She and Coleman were married, and Rachel was pregnant soon afterward. The baby came weeks before Coleman's vicarage ended in Indiana and they were preparing to move back to St. Louis.

While Coleman finished his seminary studies, Rachel worked as the Mission and Ministry Director for Lutherans for Life, a full-time job that became part-time once her daughter, Anna, was born.

"I was thinking I could be super mom and have a full-time job at the same time," she said. "What was I thinking?"

Taking on so many new roles so fast, Rachel knew God was working on her in big ways.

Christina Hileman agreed. Living far away from family in North Carolina was really a blessing in disguise.

"We really grew as a family by not actually being near our family," she said.

If you are moving with children, considering the impact this transition will have on them is critical. Yet, kids often surprise us. Often they respond to life events in ways we do not expect. The kids we think will struggle with transition the most often aren't the ones who end up needing the most attention. How easily we project our adult emotions and thoughts on them, without realizing that their little worlds are not as complex as ours!

Judy Larson's number-one prayer through the transition to seminary was for wisdom in parenting. Her oldest son had always had trouble transitioning from one grade to the next, and he kept saying until the very last moment, "I don't want to move! I don't want to move!"

Judy and her husband, Eric, naturally expected this son to have the roughest time with the transition to seminary. But he came through it just fine and made friends easily on the seminary campus. It was their younger daughter who struggled the most, missing friends she had left and crying at bedtime to go back to the home they left in South Dakota.

When the Bolosans left their

hometown in Illinois, Sherry wondered who would be the new role models for her kids. Her close friends in Illinois had been those role models for so long. These same friends had pulled Sherry herself out of her despair on the seminary lawn. They drove to St. Louis, helped her unpack boxes, and took her daughters for a day so that she could get somewhat settled. With those friends no longer close by, who would her girls look up to?

One day, Sherry's daughter, Anabelle, started crying on a bench in the middle of their kitchen in their four-bedroom apartment on campus. "I miss Schaumburg," she said. "I want to go back."

Then Sherry started crying. "I miss Schaumburg, too," she said.

Society tells us to be strong. Ironically, being strong sometimes means allowing yourself to be weak. These are big moments where God works in our lives.

Sherry did not pretend to be strong for her daughter. Instead, she recognized the importance of being open and vulnerable with her. Sometimes, we need to hurt with our kids, especially in transition times. We need to show them it is okay to be sad and it is okay to explore those difficult emotions.

Sherry wondered who her children would look up to at the seminary. In that moment, her daughter looked up to her.

"He is changing me. And it hurts," she said. "It hurts a lot. But in the long run it will all be worth it."

Rachel left her post at Lutherans for Life after Coleman received a dual-parish Call in Michigan. Now a mother of two, she has stepped back from her professional role as a deaconess, though she still uses her diaconal training leading Bible studies for women in the congregations. She recognizes there are many ways to continue to serve the church, even if she is not getting paid for it.

Emilia Buvinghausen considered becoming a DCE or a teacher. But the call process scared her. At Concordia University-Seward, she started to pursue a degree in accounting. But a New Testament class at the university had such an impact on her, she decided to switch her major to theology. She knew that meant she would eventually head on to the seminary at St. Louis or Fort Wayne to continue her studies. She had met her now-husband, Garrett, during his vicarage at a church near where her parents lived. He was a seminary student at Fort Wayne, and Emilia joined him there as a deaconess student. During her first year there – his last – he proposed. Garrett had thought ahead. He realized that, if Emilia was going to be a part of his life, she needed to be in on the fourth-year interview process and conversations about their future of ministry.

Emilia's dad, a pastor, took her on nursing home and hospital visits when she was growing up, and through that, Emilia developed a love for the elderly population. She even pursued a minor in gerontology as an undergrad.

With an upcoming wedding and Garrett receiving his call, Emilia finished her first year of the deaconess program at Fort Wayne and decided to take a year off. It was more important that she get her feet under her in marriage, she reasoned, and get a feel for life as a pastor's wife before she and Garrett addressed what having two church workers in the family would look like. For Emilia, this was a total shift in thought: she moved from a heavily academic focus to a more servant-minded focus.

"It's a strange place to be," Emilia said, "trying to figure out what to do with myself."

In the year that followed, Emilia's thoughts on her vocation has changed. She is more curious now about what the deaconess role has historically looked like in the church and what that role looks like in today's church. She and her husband are expecting their first child. With the new roles of wife and mother stretched out before her, Emilia is in no hurry to continue pursuing her deaconess studies. She will continue to ruminate and research the role of deaconess when and where she can.

These snapshots prove that, as with most things in life, there is no "one way" or "right way" to

I wanted to linger in self-pity over our decision to come to the seminary, for the same reason Erica McCarty did: if I didn't feel sorry for myself, who would? But God would not let me wallow. *No*, He patiently reminded me, *you are not here because of your husband. You are here because of Me. I was in every conversation the two of you had – together – about seminary. I know your every want, and I know your every need.*

It didn't take me long to realize I needed to ask for forgiveness, both from God and from Bryan. By pinning our decision to go to seminary squarely on Bryan, I was dishonoring him and I was dishonoring every talk we ever had about this transition. Bryan would never have taken the first step toward seminary if I was not one-hundred-percent on board with it. In all of our conversations leading up to seminary, I was supportive. Blaming him for our current temporary state was unfair. The truth was, I was not as strong as I thought I'd be, starting over in this new place. All of the newness, coupled with stinging thoughts of the life we'd left behind, was harder to work through than I had thought it would be. Satan saw my weakness, and he walked right in. That voice that blamed my husband for the hardship of transition, of starting over, was the enemy. Satan, I learned, feeds on doubt. Doubt for him is a foothold.

As I mourned for all that we left behind to come to seminary, it helped me to remember that nothing in this world is permanent. God reminded the wandering Israelites that the land belongs to Him. Wherever we are, we are God's tenants on this earth. Nothing belongs to us – not our homes, not our jobs, not even our children. Everything belongs to God.

1 Timothy 6:7 reminds us: "For we brought nothing into the world, and we can take nothing out of it."

"I always tell my husband he is my home," said Christina Hileman, "and my kids, that they are my home. It doesn't matter where we are."

Regardless of how and when a family makes that significant life change to come to seminary, one thing is true for everyone: God asks for our *all.*

Giving God all we have – surrendering our homes, our comfort zones, the stages of life we're in – is no easy feat. But to make the leap to seminary, we all must be ready to say *Yes* to Him at whatever the cost, even if we have no idea the extent of that cost.

God *uses* our moment – our emotions, failures, our vulnerabilities, our joys, and our successes – for His good.

I cherished this prayer from a summer church service during our seminary years:

pursue a church worker education or vocation alongside your husband. Trust that God is leading you, even if you can't clearly see the way ahead. If He put ministry on your heart and calls you to a church worker vocation, He will see it through – in His time and in His way!

Take all that we have – our bodies and minds, our time and skills, our ministries and offerings – and use them to Your glory. We give You ourselves that we may serve You in whatever way is pleasing in Your sight. Amen.

Deaconess and DCE
What's the Difference?

From a broad perspective, many people think that deaconesses and directors of Christian education (DCEs) are synonymous terms. While both jobs center on church work and ministry, there are key differences. Here are some:

Area of Comparison	Deaconess	Director of Christian Education (DCE)
Ministry focus	Service and human care, mercy work. Primarily works in: Mission field (foreign and domestic) Congregations Institutions	Christian Education Primarily works in: Congregations Schools Recognized service organizations (RSOs)
Age group focus	All ages	All ages (though some are called to serve in specific age-based ministries, such as children's or adult ministry)
Common duties	Care for the sick, teach, visit people in prisons, retirement communities, developmental disability facilities, and hospitals	Equip volunteers to participate in a church's, school's, or RSO's educational ministries; lead Bible studies; lead or assist with Sunday School; provide educational opportunities for congregation members across all and within specific age groups
History	1919 – The Lutheran Deaconess Association, a pan-Lutheran organization, was formed to begin training deaconesses.	1959 – Synod voted at its convention to establish an office of "director of Christian Education," to provide additional educational leadership for congregations.

	1935 – All deaconesses were trained to be nurses. 1922 – The LCMS first utilized a deaconess 1980 – The LCMS launched its own deaconess training program at Concordia University Chicago (River Forest). The program provided both undergraduate and graduate training. 2002 – Concordia Seminary (St. Louis) launched a graduate level deaconess training program. 2003 – Concordia Theological Seminary (Fort Wayne) launched a graduate level deaconess training program.[17]	In a sweeping article that considers the history of the DCE role in the LCMS, William O. Karpenko II traced the evolution of the DCE role this way: Parish educator (1980s) Teacher of the faith (1990s) Lifespan educator (2010s)[18]. 2019 – first year since the creation of a DCE directory that the number of female congregational DCEs (three-hundred-three) exceeded the number of male congregational DCEs (two-hundred-seventy-three) in the LCMS
Position held by man or woman	Woman	Man or woman
Position in the LCMS church	Synodically certified, called, and commissioned	Synodically certified, called, and commissioned

---

[17] For further reading, see *In the Footsteps of Phoebe: A Complete History of the Deaconess Movement in the Lutheran Church-Missouri Synod,* by Dcs Cheryl D. Naumann (St. Louis: Concordia Publishing House 2009).

[18] "Sixty Years of Ministry by Directors of Christian Education (DCEs) of The Lutheran Church—Missouri Synod (LCMS)," The Lutheran Education Journal (a journal of the faculty of the University of Concordia Chicago), March 2, 2020, https://lej.cuchicago.edu/columns/sixty-years-of-ministry-by-directors-of-christian-education-dces-of-the-lutheran-church-missouri-synod-lcms/

CHAPTER 6

Community at the Seminary

It doesn't take long to realize that seminary is a revolving door community. Students and their families are always in a state of flux. How could they not be? The traditional path for a seminarian pursuing a four-year Master of Divinity degree involves two years on campus, followed by one year of pastoral internship (called vicarage) anywhere in the country, followed by a final year at the seminary. All the while, the Seminarian and his family are anticipating that first Call, which again could be anywhere in the country. This means that, at any given time, some families are brand new to campus while others are anticipating a cross-country move, whether for vicarage or first Call. Still others are returning from vicarages, anxious to readjust to life at seminary.

You will meet a lot of people coming and going. You will meet some people only once. You might help someone who you'll never see again move into or out of an apartment. Someone who will never see you again may help you in the same way.

At first, all of your effort in being new to the seminary goes into learning the lay of the land. You adjust to wildly new schedules, and for many, a dramatic lifestyle change.

"Seminary is very much a wilderness experience," said Krista

Weeks, who moved to St. Louis with new husband, Kyle, from California. "We're all preparing for our Promised Land. It won't be perfect, of course, when we get there. But it's easy to be discontent when you're not settled."

Every woman who finds herself at seminary comes up against this question: Is it worthwhile to make friends, knowing that seminary is only a temporary stop? In a way, making friends at seminary seems like a no-win situation. Building relationships takes time. Yet time is one thing that families at seminary don't have much of. During the seminary years, the longest time most women are in one place is two years. And because people are always coming and going – moving in and moving out – it can seem hard to connect deeply with anyone. It's hard to invest in a community when you keep leaving it behind.

How do you create relationships that matter during this season?

It's probably no surprise that loneliness is one of the biggest struggles women face at the seminary.

Fadia Jenkins didn't necessarily isolate herself at the seminary, but for a while, she said, she did put up a wall against getting to know other women well.

"I can be a friend," she said. "I can be socially interactive. But I think I resisted being anything more than that."

Age was one perceived barrier for Fadia, because she found that she was older than many of the women she met at the seminary and therefore at a different life stage than most of them. But more than that, she struggled with what we all struggle with: it's not that we don't want friends; it's that the valuable, treasured friendships we crave are the types that take years to build.

Most of us are not experts at making friends. It's hard enough leaving the friends you already have behind, let alone thinking about new friendships that may or may not last. There are a lot of layers to navigate.

Some women, like Rachel Geraci and Juli Lamie, come into the seminary community late in the game.

Rachel Geraci's first year on campus was her husband's final year; the two were married during his vicarage year. Rachel knew it was important to be creative in her quest to meet people. A new wife and new mom who was navigating the balance of parenthood and working from home, she tried to attend Chapel on campus every day. Attending Chapel got her out of her on-campus apartment and into an active Christian community on a regular basis. It also nourished her spiritually and allowed her brain to engage outside of her baby's realm of eating, sleeping and crying.

Staying home may have been the easier thing to do. The chances of making solid, lasting connections in just one year were slim. But Rachel saw immediate benefits to being social; even if she didn't form lasting friendships, she could spend time in the present with women who had many of the same questions and uncertainties she did.

"Walking on campus reminds you that you're not in this by yourself," Rachel said.

Juli Lamie admitted that it was easy for her to isolate herself. She arrived on campus from her home in England just months before her husband, Julian, would start his year-long vicarage in Illinois. As a result, she had little motivation to meet other women on campus. She felt like an outsider, she said, not because she was foreign, but because she was experiencing being new on campus by herself. During her husband's final year at seminary, Juli spent more time with the first-year wives than the fourth-year wives. Since it was her first full year on campus, she most closely identified with the first-year wives, even though she would be leaving campus the same time as the fourth-year wives.

Most importantly, both of these women made the effort to connect with other women. The excuses to not connect were strong and valid, but they knew that pursuing friendships with other women was a better and healthier alternative.

"Dig into relationships with people at seminary," said pastor's wife Gretchen McGinley. "Don't make the excuse of 'Oh, we're only here a short time so I shouldn't get close to people.' Dive in. You're in this together! Yes, it's hard, but you're not alone, so don't try to do it alone."

It's no secret that the seminary is a fishbowl community – a place set apart and unique from the rest of the outside world.

"We're like this tight-knit bubble," said Ashley Brandmahl.

That brings with it both disadvantages and advantages. Many of the men on campus are working toward a common goal. The women and families who find themselves in close quarters with others on the seminary campus can easily fall into comparison games, holding up their lives to the perceived lives of those around them. Weary moments of frustration easily creep in when you've heard or talked about a common struggle for the hundredth time. It is easy to lose our compassion for others.

Yet there are huge advantages to being in a community of like-minded people. The community is instant; you have an immediate starting point. Faith and love for Jesus is central. Here is a place where you can safely share your faith story and hear about others' journeys of faith. Here is a place where you can see God at work in the lives of His children (if you look and choose to see it). Often a friendship begins with the question, "What brought you to seminary?" or "How long did your husband think about becoming a pastor before he applied to come here?"

Many women quickly realized they are surrounded by women who are doing the exact same thing as they are – preparing to become a pastor's wife. That common ground is wide open for possibilities of connection.

"I think God really provided [friendship] for me," said Jamie Terral, who moved to seminary with her family from Camp Lone Star, a Lutheran church camp in Texas where her husband had served as a DCE.

The Zechs, who in their forties moved with their six kids onto campus at Concordia Seminary, shared an apartment building with three young newly married couples without kids. A few days prior to meeting those families, Melissa Zech had commented to her husband that she missed seeing that segment of the population. Where were they? Right next door, it turned out. Sharing space with people of different generations was a refreshing gift for Melissa. At the same time, the younger couples saw a role model in Melissa, and they doted on her kids.

This "fishbowl life" brings with it a special community, a connectedness you'll likely never encounter again once your husband is called to a church.

"I love how all my neighbors, we all believe the same thing," said Krista Weeks. "It's so unique."

Katie Schultz was surprised at how easily she forged friendships on campus. Beth Meier felt the same way. It is not unusual for get-togethers at the homes of seminary families to be a weekly event.

Kim Bartok found some of the strongest bonding moments in impromptu gatherings over a bonfire behind their apartment. Many nights they started a fire and invited all of their neighbors: "We're having a bonfire; come over!"

Spontaneity can be one of the most surprising blessings of seminary. If you remain open to possibilities, flexible with your family and generous with your space and resources, wonderful friendships often take root.

Pam Vogel, who told her husband prior to seminary that she didn't know how to make a friend and she didn't know how to be a friend, saw grace in people who unequivocally let her into their lives.

Michelle Knauss saw a silver lining in being so far away from family: "[At the seminary,] God brought others close who became family," she said.

This community of like-minded families, all in the same

place for the same goal, can also be a tremendous support system for kids. The bonds between kids at the seminary often form fast because they are together living such a unique experience. They have lived through a move. They are finding a new place to call "home." Already a level of trust exists among strangers, because these strangers have so much in common and are striving to keep Christ at the center. Seminary is a place where kids by and large feel safe and cared for, within or outside of their own door.

On campus, the Zechs encountered countless opportunities to connect with other families, and their children had no trouble making friends with other children who lived on campus.

"I'm a mom without the space but with a huge community outside our door," she said.

God puts people in our lives in specific seasons for specific purposes. Some of those people stay with us for the rest of our lives. Some are in our lives for only a moment. God created us for community, but He never promised that any community would be forever, this side of Heaven. Regardless of how long a friendship might last, you can rest in the knowledge that God put you

Four Ways to Earn Extra Cash at the Seminary

The likelihood of living on a leaner budget is one of the biggest hurdles that prevent families from making the leap to seminary, even when they feel God's gentle (or not-so-gentle) prompting. While scholarships and work study are solid ways for the men to earn a little extra during the seminary years, many women wonder how they might be able to bring in some extra cash while maintaining the flexibility that allows them to continue to raise children and/or take care of the home. Below are four jobs women have done while at the seminary, with great success. Along with a small financial boost, side projects like these can also help women get out of the house and into a community:

1. **Tutor.** What subjects did you excel at in school? Consider using those gifts of the past to help a current student, or group of students. You can post simple flyers for your services on community boards, in coffee shops and around the seminary campus. Don't forget to reach out to schools, as well, to let them know you are available and willing to work with students.
2. **Clean houses.** Often people with connections

to the seminary seek someone to help with light housework and cleaning. These jobs are made known through the seminary job boards, Facebook posts and old-fashioned word of mouth. Kelsi McGinley saw both the material and immaterial rewards of cleaning houses for elderly people. "It filled a need, got me out of the house for a few hours each week," she said. What's more, by showing up to these people's homes, Kelsi provided a small opportunity of community for people who often did not leave their homes. She brought her children with her occasionally, which allowed them to see her spirit of service and work and gave them their own opportunities to show God's love to others. Sometimes, Kelsi brought treats with her.

3. **Remote assistant.** Christine Schuetz searched for remote positions on a site called Upwork, which matches specific talents and skills with companies remotely across more than seventy categories of work. Christine found a full-time job working

together in His perfect timing, for His purpose.

During our first summer in St. Louis, I signed up our boys for a Vacation Bible School at a church near the seminary. For five days straight, I brought them to VBS and stayed at the church during the VBS program to meet people and help out where I could. That's where I met Sara, a local Lutheran School teacher whose son was the same age as mine. Our boys became fast friends, and so did Sara and I. Sara knew that my family's time in St. Louis was short-lived. But she was willing – even eager – to pursue a friendship anyway. We both knew we were taking a risk. We could do life together for a little while, but then what? Neither of us knew, but we both saw the risk as one worth taking.

Sara grew to be one of my closest friends in St. Louis. She opened up to me about her struggles, and I opened up to her about the temporary nature of seminary life. We knew our friendship might not be forever, but we also knew that anything was possible. God blessed both of us as we took the risk and invested time in relationship-building.

At a women's retreat on the seminary campus, Heidi Goehmann reminded us that you can put a lot of energy into something and not hold onto it forever. That is seminary, in a nutshell.

My dynamic friendship with Sara was an act of boldness, on both of our parts. We made the decision to invest in each other based on what we could see, not on what the unseen future held for us. Make decisions based on what you know, not on what *might* happen down the road. We only have the present.

Kelsey Fink learned not to put her own time constraints on relationships. During her second year on campus, she became close friends with Chelsea, the wife of a PhD student from Australia. Chelsea and her husband planned to be on campus for only a year or two before returning overseas. It would have been easy for either Kelsey or Chelsea to not pursue a friendship, because their time on campus was so brief.

"But God is not limited by time in our relationships," Kelsey said.

Kelsey and Chelsea continued to stay connected online after Chelsea moved back to Australia. Even from a distance, they've been able to share major milestones such as birthdays and births of children with each other.

Through seminary, Kara Johnson has realized how God empowers us to

remotely as a recruiter/executive assistant for an IT company. The beauty of remote positions is that you can choose your own hours, which allows you added flexibility at home around your husband's always-changing schedule. As a bonus, physical location is not an issue. You can work from anywhere!

4. **In-home childcare.** Often seminary wives are offered opportunities to care for children outside of the seminary community. Families outside of the seminary love hiring seminary wives to care for their children, because they trust that these women have a solid grounding in family values and faith and a strong spirit of love and service toward others. According to Kim Gradberg, these families pay well, too. Moreover, seminary families often seek other seminary families to care for their children. Beth Jones, a mother of three who worked full-time while her husband was at the seminary, recognized the mutual benefit in paying another seminary wife to babysit her kids: Beth knew her

children were in good hands while she was at work, and her family could financially help the family who cared for her children.

"There's quite a few people who want to earn money," Beth said. "[Babysitting] helps them, and it helps me, too."

create connections with others, even in unexpected places.

"Our hearts have grown to love more people," she said.

Even though the seminary fosters a strong sense of community, it is not the only community you will experience during your husband's years in school. Think of the communities you are a part of. You have a community at home. You have a community outside your door (whether you live on or off campus). You have a community in the church you attend, and you may have a community in your workplace or through a school a child attends.

"There were so many communities I was a part of," said Coreen Jander, who lived off campus. "I wanted to use my gifts in the right places."

For Coreen, this meant focusing on putting many of her gifts into a few places, rather than a few of her gifts into many places. Coreen chose to put less effort into the seminary community and more effort into her neighborhood and school her children attended. At the same time, she recognized that if she didn't plug into seminary at all, her own needs as the wife of a Seminarian might not be met. It's easy to feel less connected to campus if you don't live there.

Coreen sought advice from a friend who had gone through seminary a few years earlier. That friend, it turned out, had gone through a very similar struggle.

Similarly, Jenny Price invested much of her energy into knowing her neighbors off campus. She believes that God prompted her and her husband, Nick, to live off campus, enroll their kids in public school and get to know people in their neighborhood.

On the playground one day, she met Holly. Jenny learned that Holly and her husband were not necessarily Christian, but considered themselves spiritual.

Two years later, Holly and her husband attended Nick's ordination. Then, they started going to church.

"We met these people randomly at the playground," Jenny said. "The Holy Spirit shined through."

Community at seminary comes down to this: we are all women of courage. We are brave, all of us. We were bold enough to follow our husbands to this place, and we were bold enough to trust God's lead.

Trusting is easy, of course, when things go our way. Trusting becomes a lot harder in the dark and

Resident Field Education

Moments of Practice for Ministry

In 1945, Concordia Seminary in St. Louis launched a new short-term student field worker program. Area churches could apply to have a student work from July through September, for a minimum of eight weeks and a minimum of forty hours per week. Applications would be filled in the order they were received.

In a letter to churches, Rev. Theo W. Schroeder, Director of the Field Work Office, wrote "Our boys at the seminary need this invaluable contact, not only with the seminary professors, but with the men active in the ministry ... In your informal conferences with the lad, in your guiding and directing him, you will find new opportunities to revaluate [sic] and think through your own present ministry."

Part of your husband's seminary experience will be to serve as a field worker in an LCMS church. Men are assigned to churches based on experience, area(s) of focus and church ministry needs. As a resident field worker, your husband will learn and have practice with various aspects of a church service, including liturgy, communion distribution, Sunday school and Bible study leadership, worship planning, and worship preparation. Some churches require field workers to fulfill certain ministerial duties, such as visiting a nursing home regularly or overseeing a weeknight service. Fieldwork expectations differ across churches. Your husband may well preach his first sermon at his fieldwork church.

Fieldwork is an important but somewhat disengaged part of a seminary education. As involved as field workers are in congregational leadership, they have little say or influence over the decisions and lay leadership of the church. As a fieldworker family, you are not technically members of the church you are serving. You can't vote, and you can't serve on any boards of the church.

Perhaps the greatest reward of being a field worker is that you gain new perspectives and ideas from various churches. You might find that the way your home church handles Sunday school, for example, is completely different than how your fieldwork church handles Sunday school. You might encounter a particularly strong ministry in your fieldwork church that you never knew existed. You will learn how different churches do things differently.

The resident field education experience exposes seminarians and their families to a variety of worship and preaching styles. Use this time to observe and test the waters of service. Don't be afraid to make connections, ask questions or get involved. If you remain open and hungry to learn and gain new perspectives, your fieldwork

difficult moments – loneliness, doubt, uncertainty about the future. Starting over puts us in a place of re-building. But that place is ripe for opportunity if we choose to see it as such.

Heidi Goehmann suggests four ways of connecting:

1. Cry out to God
2. Walk up to one person
3. Be awkward and let others be awkward
4. Start the conversation

I would add a fifth way to connect: choose one thing. Join one Bible study or participate in one intramural sport or start one small group. One thing is manageable, and it can help you stay consistent, focused and committed.

Consistent participation can build relationships.

I was excited to be living in a faith community where I could openly explore and talk about faith with like-minded people. Sure, I had insecurities. But I knew everyone else did, too. I didn't know it at first, but God was using the women around me to help me gain a more solid footing in my own walk with Christ.

We are all risk takers, coming to seminary. We know we are leaving behind the familiar for a new journey whose endpoint we can't see. Embracing the exciting and the scary with others who are in similar shoes makes the journey 100 times more rewarding!

church will be a tremendous blessing to you!

Above all, don't lose sight of the importance of worship. Your fieldwork church is where you will continue to sing praises, grow in faith and stand in awe of Christ and what He has done for you. Recognize that you are a part of God's family in this place, and worship Him with your brothers and sisters in Christ, even if you don't know their names.

CHAPTER 7

Contentment and Sacrifice at the Seminary

What does it mean to be content? That question hung in the air at seminary, surfacing at retreats and women's events and even at impromptu coffee dates with friends. "Contentment" felt to me like a four-year theme, a state of being that the women, especially, were reaching for: What is it? How do we achieve it, especially in the midst of the transitory experience that is seminary? If we ever achieve it, how do we hold onto it?

Why is the focus on being content so front-and-center during the seminary years? Contentment is especially difficult at the seminary, because you are constantly preparing for and anticipating what is to come. You can't fully settle in or settle down.

This state of temporary made Beth Kegley angry early on.

"I felt like seminary was going to be like putting this strange bookmark on our lives that we would come back to later," she said.

Saying *yes* to seminary meant saying *no* to other things she wanted right then: financial security, having children right away, vacation, a dog.

I had to continually buck the disappointment that, after ten years of marriage, we still were not "settled" anywhere. As I thought about what it means to be content, I kept bumping up against my mighty struggle with seminary: God continuing to say "no" or, maybe more appropriately, "not yet," to my prayer that our family could put down roots somewhere. Our life, from the time we were married to the present, was a series of starts and stops – starting life in one place only to pick it up and move it a few years later to another place. This continual cycle of starting over meant that we couldn't dig deep anywhere: only peripherally did we belong anywhere. I had met so many wonderful people over those years, in Indiana, Kansas, Nebraska, California, and now Missouri. I had stumbled upon friendships I wanted to maintain. I had met people who I wanted to do life with. I became involved in community service projects I wanted to continue to support. Constantly pulling up roots just to stick them somewhere else was downright exhausting. Why couldn't we just *be* somewhere and stay there?

For Michelle Knauss, seminary brought periods of depleted energy and exhaustion.

"There were so many times I was tired," she said, "tired of trying to figure it out."

Because we want control, we are always wondering about the future. Asking yourself *what if* almost becomes a game at the seminary: *What if my husband is called to a church in a part of the country we've never been? What if he is called to a church in his home state, or mine? What if our future church provides a parsonage? What if it doesn't?* The questions are never-ending, because the possibilities are so far-reaching.

But constant questioning is exhausting. It takes our focus off of the *now* and puts it in a place we can't fully see or comprehend. The constant search for something more or better is like a treadmill: we use up a ton of energy and we don't get anywhere.

There are many ways to think about contentment. No one I talked to was surprised I brought up this subject, because it plays into just about every aspect of life at the seminary. If we cling too much to the past or look too often toward the future, we miss the rich opportunity to consider how God is working in the present.

Erica McCarty said that for her, contentment used to come from a selfish place. Often, her contentment or lack of contentment was driven by her own abilities to accomplish specific tasks. Her years at the seminary showed her over and over again that life seldom follows the trajectory you have planned, but that doesn't mean God is not blessing it.

God provides through means. But not always does He provide through the means you expect.

Hope Scheele admits that, prior to coming to seminary, she equated contentment with financial security. Her family could do what they wanted without worrying too much about money. At seminary, they had to be more cognizant of what they were spending. But Hope never felt like her family was missing out on important things. Being more cognizant of finances did not destroy her contentment; it actually reinforced her security in Christ. Financial security is good, but even more important is resting in the faith that God will provide your every need.

Hebrews 13:5 says, "Keep your lives free from the love of money and be content with what you have, because God has said, 'Never will I leave you; never will I forsake you.'"

Kristin Bayer saw this firsthand when she and her husband sold their home and left their beloved community in New York for seminary.

"Being stripped of what you have helps you better realize that your treasures are in heaven," Kristin said. "I love the way we've been loosened of the things we think are important."

God doesn't promise us that the road will be smooth. But He does promise us that He will be with us every step of the way. He promises to be with us during times of imbalance and during times when everything feels out of control. He also promises to be with us when life feels more in balance.

At the seminary, I had to hold myself in check constantly, being careful to not ignore the present, even as we were contemplating what the future held. I would catch myself thinking or even saying things like, "When we start doing ministry ..."

But we were already doing ministry, if we were allowing God to work in us in the day-to-day. Life didn't stop because my husband was at seminary. Our interactions with others weren't put on hold because my husband was in school full-time. I reminded myself over and over not to think about our work in God's kingdom as happening AFTER seminary. God was using us, even now. Even now, when my writing career was more or less on the back burner. Even now, when I was less flexible as a parent but was providing a solid source of income for my family. Even now, as He worked through the seminary to shape my husband for pastoral ministry.

I could not rush God's plan. Today, whatever was before me, was no less important than any day down the road when my husband would be working as a pastor. God was working, even now.

In Matthew chapter 6, Jesus tells his disciples not to worry.

> "Therefore I tell you, do not worry about your life, what you will eat or drink; or about your body, what you will wear. Is not life more than food, and the body more than clothes? Look at the birds of the air; they do not sow or reap or store away in barns, and yet your heavenly Father feeds them. Are you not much more valuable than they? Can any one of you by worrying add a single hour to your life?
>
> "And why do you worry about clothes? See how the flowers of the field grow. They do not labor or spin. Yet I tell you that not even Solomon

in all his splendor was dressed like one of these. If that is how God clothes the grass of the field, which is here today and tomorrow is thrown into the fire, will he not much more clothe you—you of little faith? So do not worry, saying, 'What shall we eat?' or 'What shall we drink?' or 'What shall we wear?' For the pagans run after all these things, and your heavenly Father knows that you need them. But seek first his kingdom and his righteousness, and all these things will be given to you as well. Therefore do not worry about tomorrow, for tomorrow will worry about itself. Each day has enough trouble of its own."[19]

Balancing student life with family is one of the biggest challenges of seminary. The life of a seminary student is intense – and theological studies are both deep and time-consuming. The things we give up to come to seminary often play into the health of family relationships at seminary. Jamie DiLiberto admitted she didn't realize how much time-consuming work seminary required until her husband was in the thick of his first year. When he felt stressed, Jamie did, too. Time management and course load were the two biggest struggles for her family at seminary.

"Marriages do undergo tension here," said Dr. Tim Saleska, the Director of Ministerial Formation at Concordia Seminary in St. Louis.

Long hours of reading and studying for class often pulls the men away from their families. When this happened to David Jander's family, both he and his wife, Coreen, questioned whether being at seminary was healthy for their family or their marriage. Ultimately, each time they questioned, they realized that Satan

---

[19] Matthew 6:25-34

was manipulating the natural challenges of the seminary life to cause them to question David's – and his family's – calling.

"I found I had to remain aware of what God was giving us in this place so I could remain grounded in the truth that this is the journey He brought us on to glorify Him and serve one another," Coreen said. "If I spend too much time considering what I lost in coming here, I am not allowing myself to be used in this new community."

It's true that God asks a lot of us when we make the leap to seminary. But what He asks us to give up is only a trade-off for something better. Of course, we can't see what that "something better" is. And that's where He asks us to trust Him.

Kara Johnson traded in a job she loved as a graphic designer to move with her family to seminary. She thought she would find another job in graphic design while her husband was in school full time. But no job opportunities panned out. The Johnsons had two young children, and Kara never saw herself as a stay-at-home mom. Yet with no open doors to a job at seminary, she began to think that God was asking her to use this time to simply be with her kids.

During the more mundane everyday moments, Kara made a conscious effort to lean into contentment. As she washed the dishes, she would ask herself, *How can I be content in this moment?* And she would pray for the adult or child who made that dish dirty, even if she was washing the dish for the third time that day.

Like Kara, Beth Kegley knew that, through seminary, God was telling her "not yet" to some of the things she most desired. She focused on making the slow and even seemingly boring days of seminary life matter.

Women's Formation at the Seminary

How do We Grow in Faith Alongside Our Husbands?

Who am I in this process? What does God have in store for me? How does my faith journey compare to my husband's?

These are some of the most common questions that confront women at the seminary. Our husbands dedicate years of theological study to the Bible's foundational languages and big questions such as, "Who is God?" "What is sin?" "How do the Gospels compare?" and "What does it mean to be Lutheran?" Meanwhile, we as women continue to question or work toward our own vocations and identities – as wives, as mothers, as friends, and maybe even as breadwinners. As our husbands are establishing a strong theological foundation for their future in ministry, it's easy to feel like we as women are being left behind.

"Your husband is working on himself and growing and learning," said Jamie Terral. "I feel like I need to keep up with that."

A lot of questioning takes place over the seminary years, about how God is shaping our identities as women and wives to support our husbands in their callings while at the same time not losing sight of our own God-given callings. Moreover, it is important that we are continuing to invest in

"Those days transformed into five[20] of the best years that were anything but boring," she said.

The Knauss family had to let go of a lot of possessions to come to seminary. Much of their furniture from their home in southern California would not fit in a campus apartment. Michelle knew as well as anyone that life is not about possessions. But she had a fetish for dishes. She treasured her collection of unique and colorful dishes – pieces that carried stories, but also took up space. If they were leaving behind non-essentials, surely it didn't make sense for her to bring her dishes along. But could she really let them go?

I think it's fair to say that most women gain a new understanding or appreciation of contentment during their time at seminary. When God tests us, He opens us up to new opportunities of trusting Him.

Trusting God and seeing how He provides builds us up in faith and gives us confidence to trust Him more.

Throughout Scripture, God comes to the rescue for those who cry out to Him. He provided manna and quail to the wandering, hungry Israelites

---

[20] Casey Kegley, Beth's husband, stayed at Seminary for an extra year to earn his STM – Master of Sacred Theology.

(Exodus 16). He provided rest and sustenance to Elijah, who was tired of running and was ready to die (1 Kings 19). He provided a second chance to Jonah, who at first wanted go anywhere BUT where God was calling him.

During your time at seminary, you will see and hear about God's provision in big ways, small ways and even miraculous ways.

Men often take on jobs to help with finances through the seminary years. There is work study, of course. But some men take on jobs off campus, too, working as gas station clerks, church music directors, DCEs, auto repairmen, and more.

The food banks on both the St. Louis and Fort Wayne campuses help many seminary families cut down on regular grocery bills. Our family went months without buying canned vegetables, ketchup, soup, or macaroni and cheese. The Re-Sell-It shops on both campuses offer household items and clothing in good and often new condition. The Adopt-A-Student program and support from churches nationwide ease the financial burden for the majority of seminary families. You will be humbled by checks that show up both unexpectedly and with regularity in your mailbox – from people you've never met.

our own theological and spiritual growth, even as our husbands are growing themselves.

If you need just one reason to be a part of the seminary community, consider this: the seminary gives you a one-of-a-kind opportunity to grow in your knowledge of the scriptures and to grow in your faith alongside other Christian women who are walking the same road that you are.

Faculty wives at the seminary have long embraced a spirit of humble service to help women process their very real questions about identity and purpose at the seminary. When Jeff and Renee Gibbs moved to St. Louis in 1992, Renee encountered a vibrant Seminary Women's Association (SWA) on campus. Seminary professors led theological and practical courses for wives in the evenings, on a volunteer basis. The classes allowed the women to get to know the professors and sample some of the material their husbands were learning. Faculty wives taught Bible studies and led classes on how to be a pastor's or a vicar's wife, as well as more hobby-oriented classes, such as quilting and sewing. Others taught stained-glass or ecclesiastical embroidery.

While there was no curriculum for women per se, faculty and faculty wives recognized the importance of encouraging the women on campus in their faith and in their vocational identities. Faculty wives even organized overnight retreats for the women on campus.

"We wanted to give this present to them," Renee said.

The seminary has long recognized that spiritual and vocational support for the women on campus is crucial. Feelings of inadequacy, insecurity and worry over not being strongly grounded in God's word have hovered over women at the seminary for decades. Some women plug in right away to the support the seminaries provide the women. Others don't, because they're too busy or too shy or perhaps even live too far away.

During her husband's years at the seminary, Suzy Brakhage struggled with believing God's promises.

"I don't feel that I read the Bible enough and I feel somewhat stagnant spiritually," she said.

Kim Bartok can relate. She admitted that at the seminary she felt spiritually dry.

"Not that I doubted God," she said. "I just felt so unfed."

Kim attended Renee Gibbs's class, "After the Boxes are Unpacked," based on a book of the same name by Susan Miller, during her husband's first year at the seminary. The class offered practical advice for transitions and helped Kim get to know other women on campus who were in her shoes. But she missed Bible study opportunities and ways to seriously dig into God's word with others. Kim's husband, Jim, loved to share with Kim all the things

Pam Vogel shed tears multiple times over how others had paid for her husband and family to be at seminary. That's how grateful she was for outside support. Being covered by other people's grace was often how bills got paid.

Melissa Zech said she wishes she had known how well God would provide for her family at the seminary. But in living out the moments where God has called them to be, Melissa saw first-hand that God doesn't turn His back when a family comes to the seminary. One day, a slew of bills came in the mail all at once. One of them was particularly large, for her daughter's orthodontic work. But alongside those bills in the mail that day were a handful checks from their seminary supporters. The total among those checks covered all but $40 of the total bill expenses.

"It blows my mind," she said. "I can't believe it."

Added Kristen Bayer: "We worried a lot more about money when we made way more of it."

The many supporters and donors to the seminary and ministry life can't hear enough about how their kindness and generosity affects the people it touches. The ripple effect from that support is tremendous. A little extra money each month, food from the food bank, clothes, household items and toys at the Resell It Shop – these programs and moments give families at seminary breathing room.

Accepting that support is humbling. I fought it at first, the sinful nature in me squirming over the thought of relying on others to get through this lean time. But then I realized that, just as He was asking me to trust Him to provide for us, He was also prompting others to give. God not only provides things for us; He provides people for us. And often, He provides things through people. Hebrews 13:16 says, "And do not forget to do good and to share with others, for with such sacrifices God is pleased." Romans 12:13 tells us to "Share with the Lord's people who are in need." If I neglected to accept the gift God was putting at my door, that meant I was relying on myself and leaning on my own pride more than I was surrendering to Him.

The wide-ranging support our family received during our four years at seminary meant that we did not have to keep such a tight rein on our finances. I worked full-time while my husband was in seminary, and not having to worry about where every penny was going freed me up to spend more time with our kids when I was home.

No one has to support any of us. But he was learning in his classes. But Kim, who took care of their three young children at home and a few other children, as well, couldn't experience the same level of enthusiasm over deep theological concepts. She knew that God chose her husband for ministry. But she started to wonder, "Did God choose me?" How could she possibly have a role in ministry life if she was so spiritually starved?

Over and over she came up against this question: What does it mean to be a child of God? In weaker moments, she questioned whether she was chosen as God's child. It was obvious her husband was, but what about her? In her heart, she knew she belonged to God and God claimed her as His. But she felt desensitized about what it actually means to believe in God.

"I know what it means to have faith and I am teaching it to my kids," she said.

But all the while, she felt she was at a child's level of knowing Bible stories.

During her husband's year on vicarage, she admitted, "Right now, my challenge is just begging God to help me. I can't do it by myself."

During her final year on campus, Kim not only participated in a small group Bible study; she led it, with the help of resources provided by Families in Transition (FIT) team. The FIT team was organized in 2013 following a series of robust conversations between faculty members, faculty wives, and seminary wives about how to more intentionally involve and engage with women campus.

The proposal committee identified four components to a successful and ongoing curriculum for women:

- Formation
- Growth
- Mentoring
- Community

"We were trying to do something that had not been done," said Celina Haupt, wife of Concordia Seminary's Associate Provost and Assistant Professor Ben Haupt.

The community component had existed for decades, as the wives of faculty members were focused on interacting with and bringing together the women on campus. But were there also specific ways to encourage formation and growth, as well as find and connect with mentors?

Addressing those questions required a team of out-of-the-box thinkers.

As the committee thought about how to build these four components into a new curriculum for women, they reached out to pastors' wives. They particularly focused on women who had been in the parish for less than ten years. The committee distributed surveys, asking questions like, "How did you feel in your husband's first Call?" "What do you wish you had known prior to your husband's first Call?" "Did

God works through others to provide for us.

Along with financial resources, you will be humbled to learn that people who you don't even know are praying for you. That is no minor thing. We saved cards and letters from congregations and individuals across the country who gave us a peek into their lives and shared with us that they were regularly lifting us up in prayer.

Christian author Ann Voskamp writes: "The world needs prayer warriors who don't see prayer as the least we can do but the most we can do."

It seems counterintuitive, but contentment and sacrifice go hand-in-hand. Without sacrifice, we wouldn't cry out to God. Without challenge, we would not appreciate contentment. Without suffering, we wouldn't realize our need for a Savior.

Paul encourages believers to commend themselves as servants of Christ, whatever situation they're in: "in great endurance, in troubles, hardships and distresses … in hard work, sleepless nights and hunger … through glory and dishonor, bad report and good report … poor, yet making many rich;

having nothing, and yet possessing everything."[21]

Contentment is God's gift to us; He wants us to experience times of peace. But He also wants to use us in our weakness and work through our doubts and troubles.

Michelle Knauss arrived at the conclusion that being content was living at peace with who God made her to be. Because her fetish for dishes is part of who she is, she reasoned it was okay to enjoy them and keep them for herself. Her family gave up many beloved possessions to come to the seminary, but her dishes weren't one of them.

In times of exhaustion, longing to be at peace in the present without thinking about what comes next, Michelle took comfort in the words of Isaiah 40:28-31:

> Do you not know? Have you not heard? The LORD is the everlasting God, the Creator of the ends of the earth. He will not grow tired or weary, and his understanding no one can fathom. He gives strength to the weary and increases the power of the weak. Even youths grow tired and weary, and young men stumble and fall; but those who

you feel supported during your time at seminary?" and "What would have been helpful during your time at seminary?"

All in all, the goal of the new FIT team was to provide opportunities to better equip women for life on campus and life in the church. Celina took on the newly created role of Women's Coordinator at Concordia Seminary, followed a few years later by faculty wife Katie Nafzger.

In Fort Wayne, seminary wives still gather regularly for evening classes taught by seminary professors. Faculty wives volunteer as advisors for the Seminary Women's Assembly (SWA) and often lead and participate in events for seminary wives.

This is what makes the interactions between faculty, faculty wives, and women at the seminary so integral. Organized classes are one way of helping wives feel more connected to the work their husbands are doing and how they as women fit into the picture at the seminary.

In Fort Wayne, Kelsi McGinley found that the women's classes helped to give her a more solid grounding of what it means to be Lutheran.

"They definitely put stuff in layman's terms for us," she said.

But, Renee Gibbs added, this is where small group gatherings can also reap tremendous benefits.

"That's where you can really

---

[21] 2 Corinthians 6:4-10 (portions)

support each other and pray for each other," she said.

Our husbands grow so much at the seminary. It is important that we, as their helpmates, grow, too.

"For health in ministry, the research is totally clear," said Dr. Tim Saleska, who oversees the Women's Coordinator position at Concordia Seminary. "It's not theological problems that undermine a ministry; it's the relational."

The seminary campuses offer multiple and ongoing opportunities to encourage women in their quests to grow and mature in their faith. Retreats, evening classes, small group Bible studies, social events and even special events for couples are all geared toward equipping women to walk confidently in their faith in Christ, building each other up and encouraging one another.

"We care for the women," said Renee Gibbs, "and we always have."

hope in the LORD will renew their strength. They will soar on wings like eagles; they will run and not grow weary, they will walk and not be faint.

"I don't have to find my own energy," she said. "God's going to lift me up."

When we consider the resources He offers us, the many ways He loves us, and His will for us, we stand a greater chance of living in contentment, in this season and always.

CHAPTER 8

Faith in Your Role at the Seminary

Before we came to seminary, I had wrestled with the push-and-pull of my multiple roles: wife, mother, writer. I was a mom with one foot at home and one foot on the professional stage. After a lot of reflection and many attempts and failures, I had finally found my niche as wife/mother/writer. Our life as a family was almost perfect. The only missing piece of the puzzle was that my husband was not happy in his job – AND he had this persistent urge to leave his career as an engineer and go into the ministry.

When we arrived in St. Louis, I thought there was still a chance I could achieve that perfect balance. Was it possible to continue my freelance career and be present and flexible for my children while my husband went back to school full-time? My husband understood my desire to do that, but he felt that my seeking full-time work was more financially responsible. I applied for full-time jobs, including a job I had never heard of – translation project manager – that had shown up as a skills match on my Monster.com profile. Even as I filled out applications, I continued to challenge my husband that perhaps God was asking us to step out in faith and watch Him provide through my freelance work and stay-at-home lifestyle.

I'd thought I'd heard God's voice: *take a risk. Trust me. I'll take care of you.*

The question of what I would do during my family's four years at seminary really came down to a question of finances. How much financial security were we willing to risk? Was the value of not working full-time and staying home with my kids worth taking out student loans? How could we be wise with the major decisions before us?

Our answer came down to a coincidence we could not ignore. The job I was offered as translation project manager was within walking distance of both our home and the seminary. This was God's way of providing for our family.

Take a risk. Trust me. I'll take care of you. God's voice was leading me to trust Him by putting my freelance career on the back burner for a time.

Every family faces hard questions about vocation as they transition to seminary. There is no one-answer-fits-all approach. The women I interviewed for this book represent just about any trajectory you can think of:

- stay-at-home parent to full-time employee
- full-time employee to stay-at-home parent
- full-time employee to full-time employee
- stay-at-home parent to stay-at-home parent
- wife to new mother
- wife who works full time, longing for children of her own
- empty nester who works full time
- empty nester who stays home

Regardless of where you fit in this list, you have at least one thing in common with everyone else: how you spend your days during the seminary years will look different than how you were spending your days prior to seminary. Seminary represents a change of direction for all of us. How do we embrace this change and not beat ourselves up, trying to stay the course with God's plan for our family?

Kara Johnson was sure she would continue to work outside the home as a graphic designer once her family made the transition to seminary. But she was not able to find a job in her field. With no job, she poured her time into her role as a young mom.

"I hadn't realized how much value of my identity I put into what I did [as a career] until I moved to St. Louis," she said. "God has used this time as a transition piece for me to realize my place right now is at home. Before, I would not have thought it was my dream to stay home, but it has become a dream."

Kelsi McGinley left a job as an accounting specialist for a mortgage company to stay home with kids once her husband started seminary. Her own mother was a stay-at-home mom, and Kelsi was sure she would never do that.

"I was contributing to our family [finances,]" she said. "Then we came here, and [people asked], 'What do you do?' I felt like I was lazy and I wasn't contributing."

During her time at seminary, Kelsi took on side jobs to pull in a bit of extra cash. She cleaned houses for elderly couples once a week, and she offered alterations and sewing services for seminary families and for the chapel.

Jeff and Fadia Jenkins showed up to seminary as empty-nesters. Their decision to come to St. Louis had largely rested on Fadia's career in the specialized medical field of transplants. Fadia had worked for many years in the transplant department at a hospital in Oklahoma. But her specialized position wasn't available just anywhere. When she learned that St. Louis had a transplant department – and was then offered a job there – she felt that God was opening a door for her and Jeff to move to St. Louis.

"My job in a sense defines me," said Fadia, "because I've been doing it for so many years. It's what I do, and I enjoy doing it."

Still, in St. Louis, Fadia wrestled with major spans of discontent and doubt in her job – not because of the job itself, but because of her coworkers. For the first time in her life, she was beginning to not enjoy the work she did. But was there an alternative? If she didn't work in a transplant lab as she had done for the past thirty years, who was she? What else would she do with her time and her life?

Some days she would bring home acute frustrations, and friction would press on her and her husband. She would question why they were at seminary and why she had to leave the job she loved in Oklahoma.

"It was playing with my head," she said, "making me feel like we were in the wrong place."

She questioned, "How do I fit into this picture anymore?"

We often don't realize how much we define ourselves by the work we do until that work is in tension with other parts of our lives. When your identity seems to be in conflict with everything else in your life, then what?

Over time, Fadia saw that the discontentment she felt could actually be God at work. Through the challenges, she began to wonder if God was preparing her for something else.

"It started to make me think that maybe there's more to me, too," she said.

What we give up in a major transition begins to change our identity. This is a conversation that plays out over and over again on the seminary campuses.

Jenny Price, who was passionate about teaching, considered a job offer at a middle school when her husband, Nick, started seminary, but the job was part-time. Financially, it didn't make sense for her to take the job because their family would be spending more on childcare than what she was able to bring in.

Jenny remembers a jarring realization as she weighed that job option.

"Wait a minute!" she thought. "I know Nick's calling, but what about mine?"

She realized she had to think about her vocation differently.

"I had to make choices," she said. "Does what I do equal who I am?"

With two young kids and another on the way, she shifted course. She would spend the seminary years as a stay-at-home parent and tutor in the evenings and on weekends.

Seminary presents a unique window of opportunity for women. It is a time to experiment with different roles – stay-at-home parent, full-time employee, remote contract worker – knowing that those roles are only for a time. During the seminary years, you have an opportunity to seek God's guidance and perhaps do something completely new in a new place. Be excited, always asking how God might be working in your life and in the lives of those around you.

Many women feel strongly called to fully embrace their role as a stay-at-home parent during their husbands' seminary years. Judy Larson was content in her role as a stay-at-home mom prior to coming to seminary. It was important to her to hold onto that role at the seminary. Juli Lamie never had a strong drive for a particular career. For a long time, she fought anxiety over how she could contribute to the world. She always wanted to be a mom, but was that enough? Juli thought she needed more to define her.

"I don't think the secular culture really values being a mom or a wife," Juli said. "Yet, raising children is no small thing. It's such an important job and has such an impact on society."

Seminary provides a unique training ground for parenting. At any given time, the campuses hum with young women who are finding their way through the beautiful and messy role of motherhood. Many are new moms who are still learning the ropes.

"I feel like seminary was one of the best places to learn how to be a mom," said Jamie DiLiberto. Jamie and her husband, Anthony, came to the seminary with their two-month-old daughter. Jamie remembers struggling with loneliness in this new place, while simultaneously figuring out what this role of motherhood looked like.

She found solid camaraderie with other moms on the playground and elsewhere on campus. Some of the moms were older than she, others around the same age. As these women interacted with, disciplined, and worked with their own kids on campus, Jamie encountered role models and insights for her own parenting. Examples of parenting were all around her – on the playground, during visits with friends, even in hearing through the walls how a neighbor handled her two-year-old's tantrum.

"It was a great group to learn from because we all had similar core values, but there were a variety of parenting styles and ideas," she said. "As we hung out … we could share problems, offer advice, commiserate and encourage each other … It helped ease me into motherhood."

All in all, seminary is a safe place to practice being a parent. It is a place where kids can grow and learn and make mistakes. It is a place where parents can grow and learn and make mistakes. For this short time, you are in a community of like-minded people who hold similar values. We all want to teach our children about Christ's love and encourage them to love others as Christ loves us. And we are, for a time, doing that together in a uniquely tight-knit Christian community.

One facet of our role at the seminary is to consider and explore what life as a pastor's wife will be like. Seminary is our time to prepare for this new role and to ask questions and to confront the stereotypes that often come with being a pastor's wife. How does the seminary prepare us for this upcoming role?

Some women are wholeheartedly open to a future role of

"Pastor's wife" and embrace it with excitement. Others are quick to say that they never imagined themselves in the role of "Pastor's wife" and weren't so open to the idea at first. In a survey for this book, only eight percent of respondents said they always imagined they would be a pastor's wife. That means a whole lot of us had some major adjusting to do when it came to facing the reality that, if our husbands were studying to become pastors, we were ourselves on the road to becoming pastors' wives, like it or not.

Most women who show up to the seminary have no idea what the role of a pastor's wife looks like. And that's okay. Early on at the seminary, I couldn't even think about what being a pastor's wife meant. I was too busy contemplating my role as a "seminary wife" and wondering how I stacked up to the many seemingly strong and beautiful women I was meeting. I was sure these women – moms and teachers and social workers and biologists and artists – were more confident, more settled, and more theologically grounded than I was.

False expectations of what being a wife at the seminary meant pressed on Pam Vogel early on. For example, she feared that other women would judge her if she did her grocery shopping at Lucky's – a grocery store that specializes in organic foods – rather than at the grocery store down the street from the seminary campus. She also feared she would be judged for her parenting decisions.

Melanie Aarsvold described how people in her workplace viewed a pastor's wife. A co-worker told everyone to tone down their swear words in Melanie's presence, because Melanie's husband was going into the ministry.

But another interesting opportunity came with being branded as a seminary wife: Melanie's coworkers started to come to her with questions about faith.

"It's like you're wearing a sweater that says, 'I'm a Christian! Ask me questions!'" Melanie said. "I wasn't wearing that sweater before we came here."

Erica McCarty admitted that her biggest struggle being at the seminary was learning to accept that you don't have to possess a specific personality or act a certain way.

"There can be this attitude of, 'This is what a seminary wife is supposed to look like,'" she said. "You don't have to conform to this cookie-cutter mold."

Erica found that God pointed her to the differences – unique characteristics that set women apart from one another – to get to know and appreciate the many women she met on campus.

"Know that God has brought you to this ministry because you bring something to the table that no one else has," she said.

At any given time, there are sixty-to-eighty women on the seminary campuses, spanning from newlyweds to grandmothers. If you're intentional, you can both learn from and encourage every woman you meet: newlyweds, new moms, women who long for children of their own, empty-nesters, women who work outside the home, stay-at-home moms, retired women, women who always seem happy, women who are resentful, women who are unsure of what this experience at seminary means for them.

As you consider your future role of pastor's wife, don't lose sight of your role in the here-and-now, as a seminary wife. Being a seminary wife is a role of exploration. You will explore what it means and what it does not mean to be a pastor's wife. Being a seminary wife is a role of reflection: How has God taken care of you and your family up to this point? How will He continue to care for you through this season and how will He prepare you for your future role? It is also a role of discernment: How can God use you now at the seminary and in the various communities in which you're involved? How might He use you in the future?

Seminary is a place to learn. It is a place to grow and a place to wrestle and a place to ask questions. Take advantage of this safe place to explore your various roles and how God is using them to shape you into the woman He desires you to be.

As you question your role and who you are at seminary, beware of one of Satan's favorite traps: comparing yourself to other women. It's easy to do this anywhere, but it's especially easy at seminary, because seminary is a concentrated community of passionate, like-minded people. You might covet someone's job, another woman's parenting skills or patience with her children, or the attitude of another woman who doesn't seem to be struggling through the seminary years like you are. Or, you might think you handle certain situations better than someone else does or take care of your children better than that mom in the next apartment building takes care of hers. You might even fight jealousy over a seminary student who appears to be breezing through his course load while your husband slogs through his.

All of this is normal — but it's dangerous. Satan uses those moments of comparison to both highlight our weaknesses and make us feel better on the backs of others' weaknesses. Because we're sinners, we measure ourselves against the world's standards and hold ourselves up to how *others* perceive us, rather than how Christ alone *values* us.

"When we arrived at the seminary, I was still the confident-looking but deeply insecure person I had always been," said Liz Garcia.

This comparison game is a constant battle. As a stay-at-home mom, Kelsey Fink spent vast amounts of time through the seminary years cooking and reading. In her daily work, she found herself constantly pushing back against society's expectation of women today. Society might define her work, the way she chose to spend her time, as "old-fashioned," "traditional," or "non-progressive." She had to push those stereotypes out of her mind.

"Every morning, you have to kill off the old Adam," she said. "Every day, you have to wake up and say, 'I am not playing that game.'"

Even in parenting, Kelsey wrestled with comparing herself to

Six Ways to Help Kids Connect

Everything is unfamiliar when you arrive in a new community and at a new church. This can be especially exciting – and especially scary – for kids. They have come to this new place by no choice of their own. They will be forced into new situations. They will wear the label of "new kid on the block" whether they like it or not. Here are six ways to help your kids connect in the wake of a major move:

1. **Sign them up for your church's Vacation Bible School.** VBS is commonly organized by age or grade, so the chances of your kids connecting with other kids their age there is high. What's more, VBS can most always use additional volunteers. You can volunteer and get to know some members of the congregation yourself while at the same time keeping a distant eye on your kiddo to make sure he is hanging in there okay. If a meltdown does occur, you are right there (or at least nearby). VBS is where my oldest son made his first friend during our family's seminary years. That friend was the same age

the ideal mom. She admitted she does not love to play with her kids – and she is fine with that.

"I did not play house with my kids today," she said. "But I read to them for a long time. We're raising different people. That's not just okay; it's how God designed it to be."

Fadia Jenkins, who was in her fifties when she and her husband moved to St. Louis for seminary, harbored a peculiar envy toward younger women on campus, because they seemed to connect with one another easily. Sometimes, she said, she wished she were younger. Faculty wife Renee Gibbs encouraged her to focus on her age as a strength, and to use her life experience to encourage and help support the younger women.

Romans 12:4-8 reminds us:

Just as each of us has one body with many members, and these members do not all have the same function, so in Christ we, though many, form one body, and each member belongs to all the others. We have different gifts, according to the grace given us. If your gift is prophesying, then prophesy in accordance with your faith; if it is serving, then serve; if it is teaching, then teach; if it is to encourage, then give encouragement; if it is giving, then give generously; if it is to lead, do it diligently; if it is to show mercy, do it cheerfully.

As women at the seminary, we have a lot in common. But God makes us different and uses us in different ways for His glory. If we all had the same gifts or performed the same work, we as the body of Christ would be rather ineffective. God makes us different and uses us differently on purpose! He needs us to fill various roles and perform a variety of tasks. Remind yourself of how God sees you. He calls you by name (Isaiah 43:1). He calls you beloved. You belong to Him. Nothing matters more than that.

Your role at the seminary is going to be different. It's going to be different than the role you had prior to coming. It's going to be different than the roles of other wonderful women you meet on campus. God is using you wherever you are, just as He is using those around you, for His glory.

How others view you and your role during this time doesn't matter. How you see yourself and your role during this time is important. But most important is remembering how God

as my son and attended the same school my son would start attending in the fall. Because these two boys connected during the summertime VBS, my son could count on at least one familiar face in the classroom on the first day of school.

2. **Be the first to reach out.** Don't be shy about inviting people over to your place or suggesting a play date with another family with kids. Most people at the seminary long for connections with others who are in similar life stages as they are. Amy Widener suggests reminding your kids how good it feels when someone comes up to them to talk. "Help them learn how to be that person for someone else," Amy said.

3. **Don't wait to enroll your kids in classes and sports programs.** Katie Schultz signed up her family for a YMCA membership shortly after they moved to Fort Wayne for seminary. Scope out city publications and community boards to find out what's going on around town (and not just what's going on at the seminary). Don't be

afraid to ask people at the church you attend for recommendations on things to do with your kids. Jump in to this new place, feet first!

4. **Stay in touch with old friends.** Beth Jones gave her kids stationery and cards to write to the friends they left behind. My boys have exchanged letters and trading cards in the mail with their friends, and one recent Sunday afternoon my son held a three-hour Zoom call with two of his best friends in St. Louis. Just because your family leaves a place doesn't mean you have to cut ties with that place completely.

5. **Give them credit.** Kids are so often more resilient than we think they are! Kimberly Cullen said she worries about her kids whenever the family comes to the edge of a major transition. But her kids surprise her, always making friends and adapting to new situations quicker than she does. So often, we project our adult emotions on our kids when what they need and want is much simpler than we imagine.

sees you and how He made you. While putting my writing career on hold and relinquishing my role as a stay-at-home mom was hard, God used me in new and different ways during our time at the seminary. I wasn't writing like I wanted to, but I was learning the ins and outs of running a small business, a skill I knew would be important to my professional goals later on. That, I had to think, was no coincidence. Transitions challenge your identity. But they also reaffirm who you are – as a wife, as a parent, as an employee, and most important, as a child of God.

Through her own major transition from full-time graphic designer to stay-at-home mom, Kara Johnson said she experienced an "aha" moment: her role as a graphic designer may come and go. Her role as a stay-at-home parent wouldn't last forever. What will never change: she is the daughter of the King.

Romans 12:2 says, "Do not conform to the pattern of this world, but be transformed by the renewing of your mind. Then you will be able to test and approve what God's will is – his good, pleasing and perfect will."

The world will have you believe that you always need more – more money, more time, more energy. It will have you believe you are not enough.

By yourself – through your own

thoughts and actions as a human being – you're not enough. But that's why Christ came.

He came so that in Him you would be enough. In Christ, you *are* enough. Whether you're a stay-at-home parent, a full-time employee, a daughter who longs to care for her family from afar or a wife who cannot have children, you are enough in Christ.

How easily we forget to see ourselves as Christ sees us, regardless of who or where we are in the world.

Being transformed is not a one-time event. It is a continual process.

"In everything we do here, we have to have an open hand," Kara Johnson said.

Let Christ be the one to fill those hands in His ways and His time.

6. **Be honest.** Let the hard moments be hard. If your child cries because she misses her friends, let her cry and don't try to be the fixer for her. Grieving is a natural and healthy part of change. Kimberly Cullen is up-front with her kids, telling them that friends will come and go in life and some will remain your friends longer than others. Give your children opportunities to talk about what and who they miss and why. Encourage them to talk about the hard stuff. Sympathize with them and pray with them and remind them that God forever loves them.

INTERLUDE

A Brief History of Seminary

The history of the seminaries of the Lutheran Church—Missouri Synod in the United States spans nearly two hundred years and covers a lot of geography of the middle part of the country. Collectively, the history has been influenced by wars and social phenomena, as well as by the institutions' students and faculty. What follows is by no means an exhaustive history; rather it is a snapshot meant to establish a foundational context for the LCMS seminaries in the United States – Concordia (St. Louis) and Concordia Theological (Fort Wayne) – we know today.

Perry County, Missouri 1839-1849

You can imagine the modest beginnings of the Lutheran Church—Missouri Synod seminary this way: picture a 16-by-21-foot one-room log cabin in the rural middle of a still-forming country. Imagine a time when "want gawked like a spectre into the windows of the almost barren classroom ..."[22] Eleven boys and girls, ages five to fifteen, received their schooling in this space. At first, the goal for this school was to prepare students for a university education, but the German immigrants who occupied this one-room cabin dreamed of establishing a school of higher learning for theological training. How might that become possible? What would it look like?

No clear synodical distinction had yet been established. In his book, *Log Cabin to Luther Tower: Concordia Seminary During One Hundred and Twenty-Five Years, Toward a More Excellent Ministry 1839-1964*, Carl S. Meyer wrote that there was "no clarity, no understanding of basic theological principles in the question

---

[22] Carl S. Meyer, *Log Cabin to Luther Tower: Concordia Seminary During One Hundred and Twenty-Five Years, Toward a More Excellent Ministry 1839-1964* (St. Louis: Concordia Publishing House, 1965), 4.

of the call to a ministry within the church no agreement about matters of policy."[23]

As the rural log cabin school began educating its young people, a church of Saxon immigrants was forming in St. Louis, eighty miles to the north. Dreieinigkeitskirche, or Trinity Church, was founded as a confessional Lutheran church by these Saxons, who had grown tired of the oppression they had endured overseas. Trinity Church was aware of the log cabin school to the south; congregation members had themselves come to St. Louis via Perry County. As church and school leaders talked, a different vision for this one-room schoolhouse took shape. With adequate funding, the school could become a preparatory school for those entering into the service of the church.

The first class consisted of eight students: three young men ages sixteen to twenty (two of whom were among the cabin's original eleven students) and five boys under age sixteen. Trinity Church voted to pay for the needs of all eight students, providing trousers, suits, coats, and cash donations in increments of five or ten dollars.[24] The students would live with their instructors or in their own homes.

As Trinity and Concordia continued to shape the curriculum and goals of the Concordia school, they longed for a tie that was stronger than a mutual agreement. Together, the church and the school realized that a synodical organization would provide a stronger, more solid basis for the institution's operation. The Missouri Synod was officially formed in April 1847. "The synod

[23] Meyer, *Log Cabin to Luther Tower: Concordia Seminary During One Hundred and Twenty-Five Years, Toward a More Excellent Ministry 1839-1964*, 10.

[24] Meyer, *Log Cabin to Luther Tower: Concordia Seminary During One Hundred and Twenty-Five Years, Toward a More Excellent Ministry 1839-1964*, 11.

did not call the school into existence," Meyer wrote. "The school was one of the voices which called the synod into existence."[25]

In August 1847, four months after the Missouri Synod was formed, the congregation members at Trinity voted that the school be given to the synod and moved to St. Louis. Trinity suggested that all congregations of the newly formed synod should contribute toward a building in St. Louis where both a gymnasium (preparatory school) and seminarium (college) could be housed. Trinity itself pledged the proceeds of its cemetery fund and hymnal publication fund toward the effort.[26] Perry County graciously agreed to give its log cabin school to the LCMS.

Students and teacher moved up the Mississippi River to St. Louis, arriving by boat. All were housed by members of Trinity while together the church and school considered how to construct a school building.

In 1849, Trinity sold two acres of its land on South Jefferson Avenue to the new Missouri Synod, for one dollar. The synod constructed its first school building, a simple two-story 42-foot-by-36-foot structure, on the corner of South Jefferson Avenue and Winnebago Street. The college was officially established in St. Louis on December 16, 1849, with nine students and one teacher.

Concordia Seminary in St. Louis became a theoretical institution. Theoretical meant that the students were by and large home-grown: they came from Missouri Synod congregations and were trained via the preparatory school system, first attending the gymnasium and then attending the seminarium. As the institution evolved, its education focused heavily on systematics and learning the Biblical languages.

---

[25] Meyer, *Log Cabin to Luther Tower: Concordia Seminary During One Hundred and Twenty-Five Years, Toward a More Excellent Ministry 1839-1964*, 14.

[26] Meyer, *Log Cabin to Luther Tower: Concordia Seminary During One Hundred and Twenty-Five Years, Toward a More Excellent Ministry 1839-1964*, 16.

Fort Wayne, 1840s

When Friedrich Conrad Dietrich Wyneken immigrated to the United States from Germany in 1838, he saw a hunger in people in America to learn about the Gospel and about Christ. Germans were also coming to America in droves: Robert E. Smith wrote that "the flood of immigrants would double each decade until the Civil War."[27] Wyneken appealed to Lutheran churches back in Germany for missionaries and financial assistance to teach Christianity to the people living in America. Wyneken received money, but missionaries were slow to make their way overseas. In 1844, he decided to train two young men in his parsonage in Fort Wayne, Indiana, rather than wait for German missionaries to arrive. Those men were G.H. Jaebker and C. Fricke.

In 1845, shortly after he began training the young men for ministry, Wyneken accepted a pastoral call to Baltimore. His replacement, Wilhelm Sihler, continued to train the young men in the parsonage in Fort Wayne. Sihler had come to the United States from Germany in 1843, feeling called to minister to American Protestants.

By 1846, eleven young men, most of them Germans who were interested in working with immigrants in the U.S., had joined Sihler in Fort Wayne. The eleven men had been dispatched by Wilhelm Loehe, a pastor in rural northeast Bavaria who was keenly interested in answering Wyneken's appeal to send German missionaries to America. From the 1840s to 1850s, Loehe gathered funds through various sources and with another German pastor established a newsletter, *Kirchliche Mittheilungen aus und über Nord-Amerika*, or *Church News about and from North America*, to raise support for German missionaries abroad. His influence

[27] Robert E. Smith, "Wyneken as Missionary: Mission in the Life & Ministry of Friedrich Conrad Dietrich Wyneken," Cocordia Theological Seminary Fort Wayne, accessed June 25, 2020, http://www.ctsfw.net/media/pdfs/smithwynekenasmissionary.pdf.

was essential to establishing Concordia Theological Seminary and connecting it to the Lutheran Church.

As more men heeded the call to missionary work in America, Sihler agreed to head a new institution geared toward producing pastors to meet the need for ministry to German Lutheran immigrants. Concordia Theological Seminary opened in October 1846. Classes were conducted in the Fort Wayne parsonage, and a four-room house was used as a dormitory for students.[28] In his book, *Prairie School of the Prophets: The Anatomy of a Seminary 1846-1976*, Erich Heintzen wrote: "In the interest of economy, the students were given a choice of bread without butter or coffee without sugar. They chose the sugar."[29]

The Fort Wayne seminary emphasized a practical component of ministry. Rather than an emphasis on Biblical languages, the classes were heavy on preaching, teaching, and pastoral care. This was the seminary for young men who were not home-grown. The students of Concordia Theological Seminary were German immigrants who arrived with some theological training and with aspirations for being missionaries on the American frontier.

Fort Wayne was aware of its counterpart institution in St. Louis. C.F. Walther wrote to Sihler of how the Saxons in St. Louis yearned for fellowship with other Lutheran believers. The two factions agreed to meet in St. Louis in May 1846. They met a second time in Fort Wayne, where they finalized the synodical institution. Fort Wayne was particularly concerned with training pastors as thoroughly and quickly as possible to minister to the

---

[28] Robert R. Roberts, "Our 'Practical' Seminary," *The Springfielder*, vol. 35 no. 3 (Dec 1971), accessed June 25, 2020, http://www.ctsfw.net/media/pdfs/robertspracticalseminary.pdf.

[29] Erich Heintzen, *Prairie School of the Prophets: The Anatomy of a Seminary 1846-1976* (St. Louis: Concordia Publishing House, 1989), 33.

"innumerable orphaned German fellow believers."[30] Fort Wayne would become the practical seminary, while St. Louis would be the theological seminary.

St. Louis, 1850s

The early classes at Concordia Seminary stuck to a rigorous daily routine, with all students expected to rise at 5 a.m. Their first hour of the day was reserved for getting dressed, reading morning devotions, eating breakfast, and making beds. Students were expected to study from 6-8:30 a.m. Classes took place from 9 a.m. to noon, followed by lunch and a free period. Afternoon classes and study periods took place from 2-5:30 p.m. Supper followed at 6 p.m., with another study period scheduled from 7:30-8:45 p.m. Evening devotions immediately followed, and the younger students were expected to be in bed by 9 p.m. Older students were expected to be in bed by 10 p.m. There was no class on Wednesday or Saturday afternoons.

Each student was expected to cultivate a small vegetable garden on campus. Reading newspapers was forbidden, as was attending the theater. Students often spent their free Wednesday afternoons visiting in the homes of Lutherans who lived in St. Louis.

Fort Wayne, 1850s

By the 1850s, congregations in and around Fort Wayne had started giving $2,500 each toward land for the seminary, about a mile east of town. The fifteen-acre property contained fruit trees and vegetable gardens. With the help of $500 from Loehe, Sihler

---

[30] Meyer, *Log Cabin to Luther Tower: Concordia Seminary During One Hundred and Twenty-Five Years, Toward a More Excellent Ministry 1839-1964*, 37.

also purchased close to one hundred acres of woods for students to use for firewood.[31]

Professor August F. Craemer, a beloved pastor and teacher who ministered to Chippewa Indians in and around Frankenmuth, Michigan, came to Concordia Theological Seminary in 1850. His tenure filled a vacancy left by A. Biewend (who answered a call to Concordia Seminary in St. Louis just ten months into his post at Fort Wayne) and A. Wolter, who died suddenly in the cholera epidemic of 1849, at age thirty-one. Craemer would dedicate the next forty years of his life to teaching at Concordia Theological Seminary.

Craemer's wife, Dorothea, managed the domestic affairs of the seminary, expecting no compensation. Indeed, Craemer had fallen in love with her while en route to the United States from Germany. He had noticed her tending to the victims of a smallpox epidemic that had broken out on the ship.

By the late 1850s, students in Fort Wayne had successfully formed a society called the Kollegium Fratrum, where they gathered to discuss aspects of seminary life and theological concerns. Among the questions they considered were, "What should be done about the younger students who went to sleep before evening prayers?" and "Younger students who did not knock on the door before entering a room."[32]

1860s

By this time large groups of immigrants were arriving in America from Germany. Missionaries in America pleaded with their communities in Germany to send over more church workers. Meyer wrote that "[p]arents were urged to give their sons to the

---

[31] Heintzen, *Prairie School of the Prophets: The Anatomy of a Seminary 1846-1976*, 39.

[32] Heintzen, *Prairie School of the Prophets: The Anatomy of a Seminary 1846-1976*, 51.

Lord, who in the first instance had given them [his son] as a precious gift."[33]

In 1860, the Missouri Synod resolved at its convention to move the practical seminary from Fort Wayne to St. Louis. The United States was in the height of the Civil War. Moving the practical seminary to St. Louis would protect the Fort Wayne students from being drafted, because Missouri offered a draft-exempt status to students of divinity. Indiana offered no such exemption.

The practical seminary moved to St. Louis in 1861. Members of the four Lutheran congregations in the city frequently invited the students to dinner and offered to do their laundry.[34]

The seminaries operated jointly in St. Louis for the next thirteen years, but with difficulty and tension. Each seminary continued to employ its own faculty. Faculty members and student bodies across the two institutions did not agree on Lutheran ideologies, academic direction or rigor. More and more, the practical and theological seminaries were growing apart, taking their own paths with differing academic expectations and educational standards.

The dissention, along with overcrowding in St. Louis, led the preparatory department of the practical seminary (called the proseminary) to move in 1874. The remainder of the practical seminary would join the proseminary in Springfield, Illinois, a few months later.

The Seminary at Springfield

In the 1870s, a new building in Springfield, Illinois, was slated to become the Evangelical Lutheran Female College and Normal School Association. But neither the college nor the Normal School

---

[33] Meyer, *Log Cabin to Luther Tower: Concordia Seminary During One Hundred and Twenty-Five Years, Toward a More Excellent Ministry 1839-1964*, 25.

[34] Heintzen, *Prairie School of the Prophets: The Anatomy of a Seminary 1846-1976*, 56.

materialized. In 1874, twenty-nine students in the preparatory division of the practical seminary in St. Louis lacked student housing. The students were offered accommodations at the new building in Springfield. A.F. Craemer agreed to head the proseminary there, promising that the building would be used strictly for educational purposes. Highly concerned with frugality, he pledged responsible stewardship. He vowed that students would have the bare necessities, which they themselves would provide.

"Students who enter into the ministry will have to do without many things and often contend with poverty and want," he said. "It is therefore most fitting that in the seminary they become accustomed to privation and simplicity."[35]

The synod soon purchased the building from Trinity Lutheran Church in Springfield for $7,474.38. A year later, the entire practical seminary moved to Springfield.

The practical seminary officially began in Springfield in September 1875 with a student body of one-hundred-fourteen and two faculty members. Erich Heintzen wrote that Concordia Theological Seminary in Springfield began "like a little cloud, no bigger than a man's hand."[36] Craemer served as president and G. Kroening, the proseminary teacher who had originally moved with the twenty-nine proseminary students to Springfield, served as instructor.

On Aug. 1, 1875, Craemer announced in *Der Lutheraner*: "Entering students are reminded to provide shirts, underclothing, bed covers, pillows, sheets, towels; also a mattress, desk, chair and wash basin."[37]

The seminary in Springfield operated under a strict schedule, with time built in for chapel, meals, classes, study periods and

---

[35] Heintzen, *Prairie School of the Prophets: The Anatomy of a Seminary 1846-1976*, 89.
[36] Heintzen, *Prairie School of the Prophets: The Anatomy of a Seminary 1846-1976*, 17.
[37] *Der Lutheraner* 21:119

even bed making. Classes took place from 8 a.m.-12 p.m., with free time between 12 and 1 p.m. A study period was reserved for 1-2 p.m., followed by more class from 2-5 p.m. Students then had two hours free, until 7 p.m., when a two-hour study period began. After study period was evening chapel. Younger students were required to be in bed by 10 p.m.[38]

The rigidity of the schedule was in part to instill a sense of discipline in the young men. But it was also to keep the men from indulging too much in life's pleasures. Craemer himself inspected the building once a week, from the basement to the attic, making sure nothing was out of place.

"The whole program was ordered like a law of nature," Heintzen wrote, "and the purpose was to produce not only pious and orthodox but also disciplined and self-sacrificing ministers."[39]

Enrollment was closing in on two hundred students in Springfield by 1883. Faced again with a housing crisis, the seminary borrowed tents from the state's military. The tents served as emergency housing for students while another simple structure of boards and tar paper was quickly constructed. Students called this structure the Sheep Stable. Students ranged in age from eighteen to thirty and comprised "all sorts and conditions of man, tall and short, full bearded and clean-shaven."[40]

Concordia Theological Seminary would thrive in Springfield for 101 years. There were no specific entrance requirements until 1918, when the Synod mandated that a minimum of an eighth-grade education was required to enroll.

---

[38] *Concordia Theological Seminary, A Century of Blessing: Concordia Theological Seminary 1846-1946* (Concordia Theological Seminary, Springfield, IL, 1946), 25.

[39] Heintzen, *Prairie School of the Prophets: The Anatomy of a Seminary 1846-1976*, 87.

[40] Heintzen, *Prairie School of the Prophets: The Anatomy of a Seminary 1846-1976*, 93.

St. Louis, 1870s-1900

A shortage of church workers is no new phenomenon. In 1889, Concordia Seminary President Franz Pieper announced there were one-hundred-fourteen calls and fifty-seven candidates. A vast church worker shortage called for intervention. As early as the 1890s, the seminary started to release its students early, before graduation, to fill congregational vacancies. Final exams were often moved up to accommodate a great pastoral need.[41] Students sometimes left for one to two months during their studies to act as interim pastors in congregational emergencies.

But it soon became evident that such a short-term interim was not sufficient for congregations who needed intense spiritual care. In response, the seminary began to assign students to one year of interim congregational support in congregational emergencies, providing a bridge of spiritual leadership until a graduating seminary class had trained pastors ready to be sent out.

In 1899, the Demostheniana group was founded on campus, a social group whose primary goal was to improve participants' public reading and speaking. Topics of discussion included "Newspapers," "Things a Minister Ought to Know Besides Theology," and "Advisability of Students Keeping Company with a Young Lady" (Meyer 117-118).[42]

Students were forbidden to marry or become engaged, as the Seminary wanted nothing (and no one) to interfere with the men's rigorous theological studies. Any time spent with women was strictly regulated. Students were still forbidden to attend bars and theaters, but occasionally they could drink beer on campus

---

[41] Meyer, *Log Cabin to Luther Tower: Concordia Seminary During One Hundred and Twenty-Five Years, Toward a More Excellent Ministry 1839-1964*, 95-97.
[42] Meyer, *Log Cabin to Luther Tower: Concordia Seminary During One Hundred and Twenty-Five Years, Toward a More Excellent Ministry 1839-1964*, 117-118.

after supper.[43] A Sunday curfew of 11 p.m. kept students from interacting too much with the secular world off campus. The campus janitor was to report any latecomers to the president.

St. Louis, early 1900s

By the 1903-1904 academic year, six students were on year-long volunteer vicarages. Five years later, the need was greater, and twenty-three students were assigned to year-long volunteer vicarages.

"The times have changed, our faith has not," seminary professor W.H.T. Dau said in 1909, at an address at the Cooper Union Institute.[44]

By 1920, Seminary enrollment in St. Louis had reached three-hundred-eighty-three. The number of vicars the Seminary dispatched had tripled from eight years prior. A committee examined necessary steps to expand the seminary and discussed the possibility of building dormitories that would house up to four hundred students, with two men to a room.

The seminary continued to operate under a rigid code of conduct. The purpose of the rules was to encourage students to pursue their theological studies diligently and with discipline enough to be well trained for their holy office of ministry. Marriage and engagement were still prohibited. In 1926, the Christian Century criticized Concordia Seminary for the way it isolated

---

[43] Meyer, *Log Cabin to Luther Tower: Concordia Seminary During One Hundred and Twenty-Five Years, Toward a More Excellent Ministry 1839-1964*, 128.

[44] "Lutheranism in America: Its Glory and Its Mission," Concordia Theological Seminary Fort Wayne, accessed July 1, 2020, http://www.ctsfw.net/media/pdfs/DauLutheranisminAmericaItsGloryandItsMission.pdf, 14.

its students from the secular world and its lack of influence on American life.[45]

Now the tides were turning. Where the seminary had witnessed a church worker shortage in the late 1800s-to-early-1900s, the Great Depression was defining its grip on America. The seminary was facing a shortage of calls for graduating students. Many students went on to be Lutheran school teachers instead of pastors.

In the 1930s, Concordia Seminary established the vicarage as a formal requirement and educational component. While formal, hands-on training was at the heart of the requirement, the vicarage was also designed to slow the output of pastors.

St. Louis Post-WWII

As World War II took hold, seminary students were drafted. Many students left their programs of study abruptly, mid-way through their programs, to join the military. Life outside of the seminary campus looked much different. Many students, after being away for several years, decided to get married.

The seminary faced a problem. Seminary students were not allowed to be married. Yet here were these men, good and committed students prior to the draft, who had served their time at war, married their sweethearts and now wanted to return to their studies. Moreover, because of the war, men were by and large starting their studies at seminary later in life, at an age quite appropriate for marriage.

How would the seminary respond to this great shift?

Not only was the potential student makeup at the seminary changing; the culture of academia was changing quickly nationwide, as well. The synod considered its stance on the marital

---

[45] Meyer, *Log Cabin to Luther Tower: Concordia Seminary During One Hundred and Twenty-Five Years, Toward a More Excellent Ministry 1839-1964,* 242-243.

status of students and ultimately contended that a student must have prior approval by the dean to be married. The seminary, recognizing the commitment and potential of the young men who yearned to continue their studies, began allowing married men into its programs. The 1948-1949 academic year was a turning point; fifteen of the students attending Concordia Seminary (or four percent) were married.

The following year saw a post-war enrollment increase. Faculty members began to recognize that marriage proposals were on the rise among students. The seminary would need to change its housing structure, and fast, to now accommodate husbands and wives. Concordia Seminary had initially been designed as a residential campus, with rooms equipped to house single men. To solve its new housing issue, it purchased some small pre-fab house kits from the U.S. government and quickly put up the structures on campus.

Following the 1956 synodical convention, an extensive list of campus improvements began to take shape in St. Louis. The last item on the sweeping list was apartments for married students. "[T]hese have become a necessary part of a seminary like ours," reads a statement in the 1956 Missouri Synod Reports and Memorials, "when the average age of the graduate will be 27." The estimated cost to construct fifty apartment units was $650,000.

It seemed that the seminary was playing catch-up with the times. Also included in the extensive list of improvements from the 1956 synodical convention were a library, a chapel, and drives, parking areas and curbs to adequately adjust to the automobile age.[46]

While it seemed the seminary was lightening its strict viewpoint on students getting engaged and even marrying, the student handbook of 1959-1960 still asserted that a single student would generally do better in his program than a married student.

---

[46] Missouri Synod Reports and Memorials, 1956, 10.

A proposed policy for student marriage came out of the 1962 synodical convention. The synod recognized the urgent need to make "definite provisions" for married student housing, for in doing so, "we shall be following the pattern adopted by practically every larger Protestant seminary."[47] While the policy acknowledged that "the general pattern of the American life has continued to encourage earlier marriage," students were still encouraged not to marry until after their second year of study. The policy maintained that it was crucial for first- and second-year students to focus on building relationships with fellow students, to foster student maturation and general theological growth. Even still, ninety students (or just under twenty-four percent of the student population) were married by the 1962-1963 academic year.

Concordia Theological Seminary 1950s-now

Following World War II, a "Conquest for Christ" campaign helped to fund the building of a new Concordia Senior College in Fort Wayne. The senior college was meant to be a preparatory institution, providing future pastors with preliminary training before they attended a seminary.

The architect commissioned to design the new campus was Eero Saarinen, who would become more well known a decade later, as the designer of the St. Louis Arch. The LCMS commissioned Saarinen for the design of the two-year senior college in 1953. The college opened in 1957. It would operate as a two-year preparatory school for nearly twenty years. In 1976, Concordia Seminary--Springfield closed its doors and moved back to Fort Wayne, inheriting the impressive campus Saarinen had designed. The senior college was absorbed into LCMS-supported institutions across the country via the Concordia University System. Concordia

---

[47] 1962 Missouri Synod Convention notes (Cleveland)

Theological Seminary has operated on the grounds in Fort Wayne from 1977 to the present.

Almost everything about the design of Concordia Theological Seminary in Fort Wayne is symbolic. The campus, intended to provide a quiet and unified environment in which students could both detach from and interact with the outside world, was designed by Saarinen, a renowned Finnish-American architect, to represent village life. Indeed, Saarinen wrote that the campus's architecture centered on the relationship between the buildings and the world. All of the buildings face west, except for the chapel, which faces east, toward the Holy Land. The bricks that comprise the buildings are diamond-shaped. Those that are laid out horizontally represent communication between one man and another; bricks that are laid out vertically (in the chapel) represent man's communication with God.

Seminex, St. Louis

In the 1970s, a schism broke out between the Concordia Seminary faculty and the LCMS at large, triggered by foundational and theological disagreements. The synod's president, Jacob Preus, moved to suspend Concordia Seminary's president, John Tietjen, over the direction of the seminary's education. Preus and church laity in general were concerned that the seminary was teaching unorthodox ideals and fundamentals. Students and faculty protested Tietjen's suspension, and a group of students called for a moratorium on classes. On February 19, 1974, the majority of Concordia Seminary students and faculty launched Seminex, or Seminary in Exile, singing "The Church's One Foundation" as they marched off of the seminary campus. Seminex classes would begin the following day on the Eden Seminary and Saint Louis University campuses.

The uprising exposed a widening rift in the LCMS, causing two hundred churches to leave the synod and form the Association of Evangelical Lutheran Churches. Nevertheless, Concordia Seminary rebounded quickly. Seminex continued to operate for more than a decade, clashing with Concordia Seminary over which institution was the official seminary and which could officially certify pastors for ministry.

Seminex formally merged with the Lutheran School of Theology at Chicago in 1987.

Today

Looking at its hard-nosed past, it's easy to see why Alfred O. Fuerbringer, President of Concordia Seminary from 1953 to 1969, wrote that Concordia Seminary was "subjected to transplanting and vicissitudes of various types."[48] Between the economical and societal challenges in St. Louis and the geographic mobility of Concordia Theological Seminary, presenting a clear and concise history of the LCMS seminaries in the U.S. is no easy task. Today, Concordia Seminary in St. Louis and Concordia Theological Seminary in Fort Wayne operate as two completely separate entities under their synodical parent. Both seminaries wholly equip men for ministry in the Lutheran Church—Missouri Synod and produce capable, theologically grounded pastors.

Further reading

"Lutheran Immigrant Churches Face the Problems of the Frontier," by Carl S. Meyer, Church History, xxix (Dec. 1960), 440-462.

Authority Vested: A Story of Identity and Change in the Lutheran Church—Missouri Synod, by Mary Todd, Wm. B. Eerdmans-Lightning Source (November 30, 1999).

---

[48] Meyer, *Log Cabin to Luther Tower: Concordia Seminary During One Hundred and Twenty-Five Years, Toward a More Excellent Ministry 1839-1964*, Foreword.

Moving Frontiers: Readings in the History of the Lutheran Church-Missouri Synod, by Carl S Meyer, Concordia Publishing House, 1964.

Seminex Further Reading

Power, Politics, and the Missouri Synod: A Conflict that Changed American Christianity, by James C. Burkee, Fortress Press, 2013.

Concordia Theological Quarterly vol 60 Nos 1-2.

PART 3

Vicarage and the Call Process

CHAPTER 9

Vicarage
A Bird's Eye View

A significant component of a traditional four-year seminary education is the pastoral internship, or vicarage. Vicarage is one year of pastoral training that typically comprises the third year of the Masters of Divinity (M-Div) program.[49] Students are assigned to work in a church[50] under an appointed vicarage supervisor (usually a senior pastor) to gain practical knowledge of the pastoral role and apply what they've been learning at the seminary for the past two years. A student can be assigned to a vicarage anywhere in the country. This is another year of transition: you could land just about anywhere for vicarage, including in your own back yard.

Vicarage assignments are based on the needs of churches that request vicars. Vicarage assignments also hinge on particular focuses or preferences of M-Div students, as communicated in thorough vicarage interviews prior to the third year. During your

---

[49] Students who are not enrolled in the four-year M-Div program typically do not complete a year-long vicarage.

[50] Some students use their vicarage year to explore chaplaincy work in a setting apart from a church, such as an assisted living facility or hospital.

husband's pastoral training at seminary, you will likely have many conversations about what type of church your family envisions one day being a part of. Together, you will consider whether your husband would thrive as a sole pastor or do better in a team ministry position. You will consider what sort of population density you prefer to live in: urban, suburban, large city, small city, town, or rural. Is it important to your family that your husband gain experience in a church that has a school? What type of worship setting do you prefer, traditional or contemporary? All of these questions are critical for determining where your husband will thrive as a vicar (not to mention later as pastor).

To ease the burden of so many transitions, some students request a deferred vicarage. A deferred vicarage pushes the pastoral internship to the fourth year, allowing students to complete all of their academic coursework on campus *before* moving on to the internship. Ideally, a deferred vicarage will transfer to a Call once the student has satisfactorily completed his year as a vicar. But a Call is never guaranteed from the beginning of a deferred vicarage year. Therefore, students who request and receive deferred vicarages take a risk; if the vicarage does not turn into a Call, then the student and his family must be prepared to move again.

Deferred vicarages also do not allow for a student to process his internship year with classmates back on the seminary campus. Combining the theological and historical knowledge with the practical application gained on vicarage is a primary thrust of the fourth year back on campus. The traditional four-year M-Div program places vicarage in the third year for this reason: completing the program in its intended order will provide the student with the most thorough pastoral education and training. As a result of this and depending on church needs in any given year, the opportunity for a deferred vicarage is never guaranteed.

Another way families seek to ease the burden of transition at the seminary is to request a local vicarage. Like the deferred vicarage, a local vicarage is never guaranteed. The seminary can only assign as many local vicars as there are local congregations requesting vicars. Therefore, local vicarages are determined on a tiered priority system. Families with acute medical needs, local specialist doctors or specific custody arrangements receive highest priority for local vicarages. Home ownership, local employment and children's school are all considered second-tier priority factors. A basic desire to not have to pack up and move is considered a third-tier – lowest – priority for being considered for a local vicarage.

The lesson in all of this leading up to vicarage is to remain open to the likelihood that you will move away from campus for a year and then return. Many men are assigned to churches in places they have never heard of: Manawa, Wisconsin; Girard, Kansas; Warner Robins, Georgia. You have to be prepared for anything. You move to this new place for vicarage, stay for one year, and then pack up everything you came with and return to seminary for a final year of studies.

Many families treat this year as a once-in-a-lifetime adventure. Everything is new again. You will be exposed to new ideas, new ways of worshiping, new opportunities for fellowship, new possibilities for doing ministry.

The advantages of vicarage are clear. Vicarage is a time for growth, both for the husband in his pastoral training, and for the family as they test the waters of being involved with full-time ministry. It is truly a year of practice; you will get a taste for what life in the church is like with your husband as a shepherd of the congregation.

Outside the seminary community, most people can't fathom this transitory commitment. There is a lot to consider. Will you bring everything you have at seminary with you on vicarage, knowing you're only there for a year? If you leave possessions behind, where will you keep them?

Will you have to find a place to live for vicarage year, or will a place be provided for you? If you lived on campus for the first two years, you will move out of your designated apartment or townhome completely. Be prepared to move into a new unit when you return to campus for your husband's fourth year. If you lived off campus, it is up to you to decide how you'll manage your place of residence during your year away. Some people rent or sublease their homes to fourth-year seminary families or other families seeking short-term living arrangements.

Will you work on vicarage? How do you communicate honestly with potential employers – both during your years at the seminary and your year on vicarage – about this constant state of transition you're in? Many women are able to work remotely for the year they are away from the seminary. Others find work on their own terms, such as cleaning houses or offering daycare. Still others choose not to work outside of the home.

How do you meet people in this new place, and how do you get to know them? Do you plug into your vicarage church, knowing you're there for such a short time? Where do you participate in the church and where do you observe?

The men, too, must consider these questions, as well as a host of other things. Finally, they are on vicarage. They are in a church setting, doing the hands-on work they have been learning and talking and dreaming about for the past two years. Finally, they are applying what they've been learning, and using it on a regular basis.

Most of these vicars are in the church every day. They are interacting with the staff and church members. They are leading Bible studies and building relationships. They are getting to know people organically through their work. The road is paved before them; their purpose is clear.

For the men, vicarage is a next step, one more steppingstone on the road to becoming a pastor. Yet for many women, vicarage year is like starting all over again.

Kim Bartok was initially excited to move to her husband's place of vicarage in Columbus, Indiana. During Jim Bartok's first two years at seminary, the family lived on campus. They would pack their belongings, store many of those belongings with family members and move with the basics to a home that was provided for them, four hours away.

Their first weekend in Columbus was packed with church and fellowship activities, an intense time for the family to familiarize themselves with the church and the congregation. Kim remembers thinking, *What will my little niche here become?*

Then, on Monday, Jim started in his new role as vicar.

Suddenly, the shock of how fast everything was happening hit Kim. Here she was, in a new town where she knew no one, with three kids in an unfamiliar house.

"Our life was in boxes and I had three small kids to myself all day," she said.

Now what?

Kim recognized she was at a crossroads. She could wallow in despair and loneliness. Or, she could take a deep breath and face the adventure head-on. As the Bartoks unpacked boxes and met their neighbors and explored the town where they would spend the next year, Kim started to make new discoveries. She learned that Columbus had a state-of-the-art library and an indoor playground perfect for her young kids. She began to recognize value and unique opportunities in this new place.

Doug Slavens was assigned to a vicarage in Michigan, a state his family knew next to nothing about. His wife, Liz, would leave her job as a Lutheran school teacher, a job she had held for twelve years, in preparation for her family's year away. They would have to find a place to live in Michigan. They would have to decide where their kids would go to school, although Liz was not opposed to homeschooling. After all, she wasn't teaching high school English anymore.

Ultimately, the Slavenses rented an apartment, sight unseen.

For them, it was a huge step of faith. They met terrific neighbors and formed friendships. They learned that Doug's vicarage congregation offered free tuition for their kids to attend school there.

"We couldn't pass that up," Liz said.

All in all, their vicarage experience was a time of tremendous growth. Liz relished the extra time she had for her kids and contemplated how she might merge her roles of teacher and mother upon returning to seminary for the final year.

Krista Weeks had traded in her ambition of becoming a DCE once her husband, Kyle, started his seminary studies. She decided she would wait on her own professional long-term goals and focus instead on how to use her gifts right where she was. She loved children and worked at daycare centers during Kyle's first two years in school. All the while she imagined someday having children of her own.

During Kyle's vicarage year in Michigan, Krista opted not to work. Michigan felt foreign to this California girl who was accustomed to year-round sunshine. She was eager to become a mom that year, but that is not what God had in store. Krista encountered powerful bouts of loneliness and uncertainty but determined she would stay busy by immersing herself in the vicarage congregation and focusing on her love of writing. She sang in two choirs that year, helped her husband start a young adult Bible study and finished a novel for middle school readers.

These few stories go to show that no two vicarage experiences are alike. Even the circumstances leading up to vicarage differ widely from one family to another. No matter who you are and no matter your circumstances, all you can do is remain open to God's leading.

We were one of several families who requested a local vicarage. We had prayed for a local vicarage throughout our time at seminary because we had bought a home, our boys were attending a local school and I was working full time at a local office. Our family met just about every second-tier requirement for a local vicarage, but still we knew our chance for receiving a local vicarage was far from guaranteed. We made our case to the vicarage director and continued to pray for God's leading. We knew prayer was our strongest resource. It was the only thing that would help us work out what to do with our house for a year if we were away and how to handle a challenging school transition for our boys. I planned to make the case to my employer that I could work remotely should my husband receive a vicarage assignment outside of St. Louis. But until we knew for sure what our third year would look like, I wasn't saying anything.

In the end, God said *yes* to our prayer to stay in St. Louis for Bryan's vicarage year. We were able to stay in our house. I was able to keep working exactly as I had been for the past two years. Our boys were able to stay in their school and build on already-established friendships with classmates. While so many of our friends were encountering heaps of change and major transitions, the only thing that really changed for our family was Bryan's shift in work and where we attended church. Still, I know the number-one question I had about my husband's vicarage year was common to all women who were faithfully accompanying their husbands in their third year of study: How did I fit into this new-to-us church? What, exactly, was my role?

No one really tells you what your role is as a vicar's wife. God designs each of us differently, and each vicarage experience is unique. Therefore, it is up to you, through prayer and conversations with others, to feel your way into the congregation and ask what God might expect of you in this new place. Some women are go-getters, anxious to jump in with both feet. Others are more reserved, and happy to take a backseat.

I was eager to get involved in our vicarage congregation. I have always seen myself as a leader, eager to step in. What types of Bible studies would I encounter in this new-to-us congregation? What would Sunday school look like? Would I meet women my age? What sorts of fellowship events would we be a part of?

Even before your husband's vicarage year begins, you should ask God to guide and bless your family's time wherever He leads you. Pray for wisdom in decision-making, for decisions big and small. Pray also for your congregation. Ask that they would see you and your family for who you are, not simply as the next vicar's family.[51] Ask, too, that you would see the congregation not simply as an unfamiliar group of people you will worship with for the next year, but as unique brothers and sisters in Christ.

Vicarage is a ministry. You should expect to feel loved. You should expect to feel wanted. You are not simply walking into a new church as a new potential member, not this time. The vicar and his family will be front-and-center of the church. This is the church's chance to help shape a man for pastoral ministry and to help prepare a family for pastoral ministry. Most churches are delighted to have a role in that training ground.

When I asked women what had been their biggest joy during the seminary years, almost all of them answered that they were seeing their husbands live out a calling that was real and God-inspired. This realization, the opportunity to see your husband at work in a vocation toward which he's been aspiring, often first takes root during the vicarage year.

"It makes me very proud as a wife to see [my husband] pursuing his passion and knowing that he will excel at it," said Kelsi McGinley.

Kara Johnson watches her husband and thinks, *You are made for this. I can tell God's hand is on you.*

Mary Magill said she silently protested her husband's first two years of seminary, even though his joy of studying the Word was

---

[51] Some churches ask for and receive a new vicar every year. Others have never had a vicar or request a vicar every so often. Vicarage requests and opportunities differ year-by-year.

plain to see. Then, during his vicarage year, she saw him praying over someone.

"It melted my heart," she said. "I knew this man was meant to be a pastor and I finally got on board. I realize now that God was patiently waiting and shaping both of us."

Anna Davis encountered a shift of her own during her husband's vicarage year in New Jersey. She realized that church work allowed her husband to be *more* (not less) immersed in everyday life at home, in ways he wouldn't have been had he worked an 8-5 full time job. He could come home for lunch. He was more involved in his kids' day-to-day activities. He was able to be flexible with his time. Anna came to see how immeasurable the small everyday family moments were.

In Iowa, Hope Scheele encountered the same thing.

"Vicarage was a welcome break since my husband had more free time than he did with all of his studies," she said.

Vicarage is an affirming time for many seminary families. It is a time of remembering why you came to seminary in the first place. It is practice ground. It gives you a glimpse of what it's like to be in the congregation when your husband is up front every Sunday.

Vicarage is practice ground. This is not only true for your husband; it is your year to practice, as well. So, use vicarage for that purpose. Practice noticing people and committing names to memory. Julie Bridgman stood by her husband after services to get to know people; as congregants shook her husband's hand, she offered her hand, as well. Practice making connections. Who does what around the church? I often used the sharing of the peace time during service to ask people's names. Practice being the first to reach out to others – not waiting for others to reach out to you. Practice prayer, asking others how you can pray for them and sharing how they can pray for you. Practice receiving God's grace, when things go well and when things don't go well. Practice active Christianity.

CHAPTER 10

Getting Involved on Vicarage

You are not a pastor's wife yet. But you soon will be. How do *you* want to be involved in your congregation when your husband receives his Call?

As a "practice" year, vicarage is a time to reflect on what you hope your future role as a pastor's wife might look like. Do you envision being part of a women's Bible study as a pastor's wife? Seek a women's Bible study on vicarage. Do you want to be active on a prayer chain? Ask to join the prayer chain at your vicarage church. Do you want to teach Sunday School or be involved with VBS? Do those things on vicarage. The more you practice and meditate on your future role as a pastor's wife, the more prepared you will be to step into that role when the time comes.

But let's be honest. You have only one year to immerse yourself in a congregation before returning to seminary. The truth is, you may simply not be able to "practice" being a pastor's wife on all fronts during your husband's vicarage year. As you spend time in prayer, ask how God is leading you during this year of practical application. Does how you see yourself getting involved in the congregation align with what God is putting on your heart?

An interesting thing happened on my husband's vicarage year.

Even though I saw myself as a leader with big ideas about how to dive into our vicarage congregation, God did not open doors for me. Time and again, when I thought I might want to get involved in something – handbells, Bible study, Friday nights with people our age – I felt God's gentle *No*.

If I had a key word to describe my vicarage experience, it would be, "observe." This was my year to watch, my year to take a backseat in the congregation and simply observe the many networks of this church at work.

Early on, I squirmed at the thought. Weren't we as vicars' wives supposed to be seen as leaders? As go-getters? As *doers*? "Observe" is a passive verb, I thought. Surely God doesn't want us to be passive in this year of practice!

But in many ways, "observe" is what the vicarage experience is all about. This is true even for the vicars themselves. Vicarage is a strange year in that your husband is an instant leader in a church but has no official decision-making authority. He can help brainstorm the church's vision, re-structure the church's mission statement or even start a new program or initiative. But because his post is only for one year, he likely won't be around to see the fruits of his labor. He can't vote on church matters, and neither can you. In church meetings, your husband might struggle with discerning when to speak up and when to stay quiet as the church goes about its business. You are temporary in this place. Your main goal should be to gather wisdom and experience for your role to come.

Even so, God showed me that "observe" can indeed be an active verb. As I continued to watch the life of the church tick along, I began to ask questions. What could we learn from this church? What could this church teach us about doing ministry? What could we learn from this congregation's strengths and weaknesses? What could we learn from how the congregation members care for each other? What could we learn about our own family, and how might we begin to shape new traditions?

Because it is practice ground, vicarage is a year for iteration – the process of trying new things and seeing what works and what doesn't work.

I felt this "practice" at work most strongly during Advent and Christmas of our vicarage year. As Christmas approached, I began to wonder how my husband would make time for his family, when he was helping to lead five church services within a twenty-four-hour period. I had grown up in a family with big Christmas traditions. With a husband in the parish, those traditions were suddenly not front-and-center. How could we still make Christmas magical and special if Bryan wasn't around very much?

Sure enough, on Christmas Eve that year, Bryan joined our vicarage pastor at McDonald's for a quick cheeseburger and fries between the early service and mid-evening service. Our boys and I had a fast and forgettable meal at home – peanut butter and jelly? Chicken noodle soup? I don't remember.

I *do* remember crying as I thought about how my parents were eating stuffed peppers and cheesy broccoli casserole at Aunt Trudy's, and how they would get to church early to set up tone chimes, and how my mom would direct the tone chime choir like she did every year, for Joy to the World, O Holy Night and Silent Night.

At our vicarage church, I would snatch a candle from the back of the sanctuary, forgetting that the only one who could possibly hold it during Silent Night was my eight-year-old son. I was playing flute in the church balcony for the service (one of only two occasions on vicarage when I played my flute).

My boys and I would share a bulletin that night, and I would occasionally point to where we were in the service, unsure if they were even paying attention. I would let my oldest son hold the candle for Silent Night, breathing a desperate prayer that he wouldn't burn the church down. After the service, we would return to a dark and empty house, put on pajamas and wait for Bryan to come home. If Bryan had any energy left, we would each open one present from under the Christmas tree. If he didn't, we would go to bed and hope he was awake enough at 6 a.m. Christmas Day to open a few presents before he had to head back to church for the Christmas Day service.

This year of practice would strengthen my resolve as a new pastor's wife as we navigated the waters of the church where my husband was eventually called. As Hope Scheele beautifully puts it, "You learn as a couple and a family what works for you and what doesn't. You learn what is priority and what you can give a little on."

Vicarage year definitely helped me to ease into my role of pastor's wife. Because of that year of practice, I felt comfortable taking my time getting to know our new congregation once my husband received his Call. Because I had already contemplated the question of traditions on vicarage, the reality of spending Christmas and Easter services without my husband in the pew was not as harsh. I had lived this reality once already.

My experience is just one example of how God works in us through this transitory year. Vicarage is a time for growth. Growth can look a thousand different ways.

Vicarage year was the time for Liz Garcia to seriously face her lack of self-confidence. Constantly worrying about what other people thought of her distracted her from the work God had set before her. She missed Renee Gibbs, a seminary professor's wife who had frequently checked in on her, listened to her fears and doubts and joys and always prayed for her. Liz wanted to be like that. She wanted to be able to wholly listen to others and offer encouragement and support when they were struggling. During her husband's vicarage year, she used a Bible app to read/listen through the entire Bible in one year. She also read a book on self-esteem and self-worth. Little by little, she began to acknowledge the positive voices in her life and tamp down the negative ones.

"Preparing to be a pastor's wife helped me to face those issues during seminary, so that I could be in a healthy place to support my husband and our congregation," she said.

Shortly after her family moved to Jacksonville Beach, Florida, for vicarage, Erica McCarty learned she was pregnant with twins. With one daughter in elementary school, she sought ways to immerse herself in the vicarage congregation. She joined her husband's Thursday morning Bible study and got to know a lively group of women who loved to play cards and called themselves the Senior Shufflers. The Shufflers taught Erica how to play Canasta, and she joined them every week. When the twins were born late in the vicarage year, the McCartys had enough diapers to last them a year, thanks to the generosity of the vicarage congregation.

You should feel cared for on vicarage by members of the congregation. When people offer to help you, don't let pride stand between you and the opportunity to receive help. "Help" takes many different forms, of course. It might be a free meal. It might be an offer to assist with kids during service. If you have kids, you will have many Sundays with them alone in the pew. It may be a gift card or donated furniture. Kyla Rodriguez met a self-proclaimed Garden Grandma at her husband's vicarage in Michigan. The Garden Grandma's mission is to grow vegetables for vicar families.

"God works through people, and you will feel His love through people," said Kara Johnson. "When people are prompted to give, they are also listening."

My husband's vicarage church, accustomed to having a new vicar every year, hosts an annual food drive for the vicar's family. The boxes of non-perishable food, toilet paper, laundry soap and dish soap we trucked home following the food drive was nothing short of overwhelming. We cleared out our basement floor to sort the cans and boxes and paper products. Our boys had a blast scurrying from one section of food to another, pretending it was a store. Thanks to that food drive, we filled a clothes-basket-sized container with boxes of pasta. We didn't add canned vegetables to our grocery list for months. We didn't have to buy toilet paper for two years.

"I loved being the heart of the church," said Kristin Bayer. "People pour into you and they love on you and they're so thankful for you."

Allow people the chance to give, and give in return when you can. Even if you can't get involved in all of the ways you wish you could, you might choose one thing. Join the choir. Attend a women's Bible study. Volunteer in the church nursery.

If someone invites you over for dinner or out for coffee, say yes. Don't be afraid to do life with these people. Don't be afraid to let them into your world, and don't be afraid to enter into their world. Take a risk.

It is far better to grieve goodbyes with people you have come to know than to have no goodbyes to grieve at the end of vicarage year. The truth about relationships is the same on vicarage as it is at the seminary: God never promises us that our friendships will last forever. Ecclesiastes 3 beautifully reminds us that for everything there is a season.

Jamie DiLiberto joined a Mothers of Preschoolers (MOPS) group at a nearby church while on vicarage in Nevada.

When Receiving Gifts is a Burden

People are often eager to give to Seminarian's or pastor's families possessions they, the givers, no longer want or need. While this might be a noble gesture in and of itself, sometimes those possessions are worn out or are in poor shape. We would like to think that most peoples' intentions are good. However, sometimes Christians can get off track, performing acts of service because those acts make them feel good or in control. What do you do when you receive a gift that is far from what you need, or a piece of equipment or furniture that is in poor shape? Here are some thoughts:

- **Accept the gift and then donate it** to a local goodwill store. We always want to hope and trust that people's motives are genuinely kind and in our best interest. If you receive a gift you do not need or want, accept it graciously, and use the exchange opportunity to get to know the gift giver a bit more. Rather than a gift-giving interaction, see the exchange as an opportunity for relationship building. You can quietly donate the gift later.

- **Accept the gift with a statement** such as, "Is it okay with you if I pass this along to someone else if we find we are unable to use it?" Perhaps you have no need for a gently used couch, but your sister does. Think out loud who you know who might benefit from the gift. Most people are fine with a donation being passed along.
- **Say "No thank you"** and explain why you do not have a need for the gift. Often people are so driven by a desire to "help" that they don't even consider the possibility that an intended receiver might not want or need the gift. Use the interaction as an opportunity for communication, where you are each getting to know the other more.
- **Suggest another place** that could use the gift more than you can. Are you familiar with charitable organizations around town, or a campus ministry or a local Habitat for Humanity chapter? What ministries is your church connected to that could benefit from a furniture, appliance or clothing donation? An

She did not confine her relationships to the church, specifically; she used the vicarage year to reach further into the community.

Early in her husband's vicarage in rural South Dakota, Pam Vogel noticed that a neighbor said "hi" to them as they moved in. That same neighbor invited their family over for hot dogs the next night.

"She ended up being a really good friend and still is," Pam said. "It wasn't a friendship that I foresaw. But God knew."

God can work wherever He chooses. He is always working within the church. But He is also busy knitting people from *within* the church to people who are *outside* of the church. Be open to where and to whom He might be calling you during the vicarage season.

On vicarage, you might find yourself asking all over again, "Who am I here?" and "How do I fit in this place?" You will wonder what to expect during this year of "practice." But don't ask yourself what you should expect without also asking, "What does God expect of me?"

As I turned this question on myself, I was surprised to find the many things He did *not* expect. He did not expect me to join the handbell choir. He did not expect me to lead a Bible study or regularly attend social events with people my age. He *did* expect me to learn by watching. He expected me to practice worshipping in the pew with two children, and to lean on the kindness and dependability of others when my husband was not available to help. I could take one child to the bathroom in the middle of a church service and know my other child was well cared for in my brief absence. I could lean on this church family, as brief as our time in it was, and they could lean on me, because in the bigger picture, we were all the body of Christ.

God puts different people in our lives at different times. Sometimes, God uses us for specific purposes, or puts us in the paths of specific people at specific times. God also might call us to be encouragers, entertainers, or distractions in grief-filled or challenging times. Part of the work of the church is to show the world what community is.

Gretchen McGinley encountered a monumental shift during her husband's vicarage year. Rather than striving herself to "be enough" in her role – as vicar's wife, as mother, as future pastor's wife – she began to see a clearer picture of grace and resting in the knowledge that "He is enough."

intended gift might be an opportunity to network. Introduce the gift giver to an organization you believe could use the gift more than you, and encourage the gift giver to inquire about that organization's specific needs.

Martin Luther writes:

> "This life, therefore, is not righteousness but
> growth in righteousness,
> not health but healing,
> not being but becoming,
> not rest but exercise;
> We are not yet what we shall be,
> But we are growing toward it;
> The process is not yet finished,
> But it is going on;
> This is not the end, but it is the road;
> All does not yet gleam with glory,
> But all is being purified."[52]

---

[52] Martin Luther, "Defense and Explanation of All the Articles," in *Luther's Works, vol. 32: Career of the Reformer II*, eds. George W. Forell & Helmut T. Lehman (Fortress, 1958), 24.

CHAPTER 11

From Vicarage to Call

Godspeed. The word leapt out at me from the church bulletin on my husband's final Sunday of vicarage. It was such an unexpected word, I mused. I knew it as a secular term, something people say to wish friends and acquaintances luck. *Godspeed,* on taking your final exam. *Godspeed,* on your upcoming job interview. But when I read in the bulletin, *FAREWELL and GODSPEED to Vicar Bryan Meadows,* I knew there was more to the message than a simple wish for good luck.

These were far-reaching words that were cushioned in grace and love and prayer. They expressed a deep-seated desire for success in our soon-to-be new venture: a brief return to seminary followed by the Call into ministry. "Success" wasn't success as the world sees it; it was the hope and longing for God to use my husband, this soon-to-be pastor, as a longtime shepherd of His Word.

The end of vicarage marks another major transition. Once again, it is time to leave one place to journey to another. But this transition is unique in that you are not moving somewhere new. The transition from vicarage to the fourth year is a return. You are going back to a place you know. Many of the questions you likely had during your first year or two on campus are not as pressing as they once were: how to afford a seminary education, how to meet people, how to make friends, how to support your husband in his studies while you find your own niche.

But in their place is a colony of new pulsing questions: What can you take from your year on vicarage to support your final year at seminary? How will the vicarage equip your family for ministry? Did your vicarage experience bring any new insights or considerations into what type of a congregation dynamic best fits your husband and your family? Call Day – the big day when students in their final year officially learn where they will first serve as pastors – is less than a year away. What do we need to know about it, and how do we approach it? How do we pray about it? What does God have in store?

The possibility of a sense of permanence is within our reach. Permanence is something many seminary families long for after so much time living in transitory roles. Yet a sense of pressure comes with that. Will your husband be ready to take on a full pastoral role? Can you be content, no matter where God leads you? What if the church where your husband is Called is completely familiar? What if it's not?

The transition back to seminary comes with its own set of emotions. The temporary status of our circumstances is front-and-center. Men clean out offices they have occupied for a year, often for that same office to be occupied with the next year's vicar. Families say goodbye to members of a congregation they have quickly come to know. The end of vicarage is a busy time of goodbyes – goodbyes to congregation members, goodbyes to church staff, goodbyes to new friends and people in your vicarage community. For some families, the goodbyes are relatively easy. For many, they are hard.

Jamie DiLiberto encountered waves of conflicting emotions as her family returned to the seminary after a year of vicarage in

Nevada. They had grown attached to their vicarage congregation, and leaving that congregation brought Jamie to tears. She was glad to be back at seminary and reunited with friends she hadn't seen for a year. At the same time, she was grieving the church community she had just left. Suddenly, Call Day and graduation were in sight. Here she was, grieving the past, trying to embrace the present and anticipating the future, all at once. Everything was happening so fast. It's no wonder her emotions were on a wild rollercoaster.

My husband's year of vicarage service had given our family new friendships, new challenges, and new discoveries. The relationships God had nurtured were on full display during our final Sunday as the vicar's family. At the end of service, Bryan hugged one congregation member after another. He knew most people by name. I still did not. Far more people knew my name than I theirs. But the fact that so many were still strangers to me did nothing to hinder their encouraging words:

"He is incredible."

"No doubt you'll be excellent, wherever you end up."

"If you preach like that for your first sermon in your church, your congregation will love you."

One woman who I'd never met said, "I pray for you every day."

I swallowed humility in large doses – and not for the first time. Through others, I was seeing Christ's love first-hand, the love that knows no limits and keeps no record of wrongs.

There were tears, real emotions wrapped around our departure from our vicarage congregation. This powerful goodbye from vicarage was another strong affirmation from the Holy Spirit: we were right where God wanted us.

Even so, as we approached the summer between vicarage and fourth year, a new cloud of loneliness hung over me. I knew change was coming – for me, for my husband, for our kids. The fresh energy I once poured into new relationships at seminary was more cautious and subdued now, as I anticipated our final year in this place. How would this year, this final year at seminary, be different?

I remember many moments during my husband's seminary years where I felt like an empty vessel, splayed open with no sense of direction apart from, "Thy will be done." That might sound melodramatic, and perhaps it is. But I found I had to keep kicking my own will to the curb. That was especially true during my husband's fourth year. The million-dollar question, of course, that all seminary families hear and ponder, is, "Where do you eventually want to live and be involved in ministry?" We had encountered that question seemingly a thousand times over the past three years. But now, the question was real and concrete. It wasn't some casual conversation-starter that we could talk about in theoretical terms. "Where do you want to be?" was a point-blank question that would soon demand a black-and-white answer. And even with that answer hanging out there on paperwork and in the back of the Placement Director's mind, we were certainly not guaranteed a move to that place, whether that place was a town or a specific district or region of the country.

After so many months of being asked this question and pondering it with my husband, I was tired of thinking about all of the "what-ifs." What if Bryan were called to Indiana, where we would be far away from my parents but closer to his? What if he were called to a rural parish? What if he were called back to eastern Kansas, a place that was far away from both his parents and mine, but a place we loved and knew well? Would we have to start over completely after seminary, in a brand-new place with brand-new people, learning the lay of the land and forging relationships from scratch all over again? I wasn't sure I had that energy in me. But I had to trust that God knew better than I did. As my restless mind tossed and turned with questions about our future and the coming change, I knew all I could do was fall back on Jesus. *His will*, not *my will*, be done.

Finally, I was starting to feel comfortable in the seminary community and in this city. I was getting to know an amazing next-door neighbor who I wanted to be neighbors with forever. Could we stay here? *Thy will be done.* I missed the Kansas City suburbs where we had come from, and I missed the crisp air and the stoic pines of the high Rocky Mountains where I grew up. Could we end up in either of those places? *Thy will be done.* How would our two boys weather the transitions to come, and how would my husband and I help them through? *Thy will be done.*

Even with the major questions that ride on the back of the fourth year at seminary, it's important that you take the time to realize how far you've come and how much you *do* understand about this pastoral training process. The challenges, insecurities, and questions you've been up against prepare you for this final year of academics and for what comes after it. You have seen God provide for you from all angles: financially, vocationally, relationally, spiritually.

Michelle Knauss never saw a hard dollar sign for what seminary cost her family. While that was unsettling at first, Michelle later recognized the not knowing as a gift from God. Why couldn't she have trusted more thoroughly that God would take care of her family? She knew He was above every weak moment and every doubt.

"I wished maybe I had just heard that more often," she said. "God definitely had a plan."

Thinking back, Michelle said she wishes she had a sign in front of her for the first two years: "God's taking care of this. Go and enjoy the day."

Early on in seminary, Anna Davis hated the easy answer to how seminary works financially: *it just does.* Now, she says she would give the same answer to anyone who approached her with that question.

"I would say, 'It just does,' because that's exactly what He did," she said.

Many of us as parents anticipate the difficulties our children will have adjusting to a new environment when we move to seminary for the first time. But we so easily forget that kids are resilient – usually more resilient than we give them credit for. When they weather the transitions with us, we can often see how the Holy Spirit strengthens them and provides them opportunities to grow, even as He is working growth in us.

Erica McCarty saw her daughter, Joy, grow tremendously throughout the four years at seminary. Joy learned how to meet people and how to make friends and how to start over – in a new apartment, in a new school, in a new place.

"What she's gained alone makes this all worth it," Erica said.

How often during our seminary years did I fret over the way I perceived our kids would respond to a transition, only to watch that transition roll right off their backs? I saw time and again that our boys were happy. They were full of energy and full of love and full of that wild mix of affection and scrappiness so normal in siblings. Occasionally I would say a prayer of thanks because I saw how God was taking care of them. Ironically, I worried about my kids the most through transition, and they were the ones who reminded me not to worry so much.

"I don't think [kids] are scarred," said Kristin Bayer of the transitional seminary experience. "I think they're all the better for it."

As women, many of us feel shaky in our own faith or theological understanding early on at seminary, as our husbands begin to dedicate long hours to deep theological study. We feel like we somehow need to keep up with all that they're learning, even as we hold down the fort at home or work for a paycheck. The seminary offers women dozens of opportunities to be in the Word together, through small group Bible studies, evening classes taught by seminary professors, daily Chapel services and semi-annual retreats. While you may be reluctant to jump in at first, by fourth year, you'll hopefully recognize the one-of-a-kind opportunity the seminary community offers you to grow in faith and knowledge of Scripture surrounded by Christian women who are at a similar point in life as you are.

Melissa Harrington said her identity as both a Christian and a Lutheran grew immensely as her husband progressed through the seminary. The more women's classes she participated in and the more her husband shared with her what he was learning, the more her faith grew.

Christina Hileman noticed that she made more of an effort to incorporate God into her daily life as she participated in women's classes and built up friendships at the seminary. That led to a more acute focus on how she and her husband are raising their children. They want Christ to be in their daily conversations and prayer to be dynamic and real, flowing out of their lives. By fourth year, their family's faith life had transformed.

Similarly, Coreen Jander watched the effects that her husband's spiritual growth had on their family of three children throughout his years at seminary. As her husband grew into a strong spiritual leader, Scripture became a stronger base for him, for her, and for their children.

Finally, by fourth year you will hopefully see how God has provided for you in your marriage. Through questioning, doubt, and insecurity He gives us opportunities to build each other up and encourage each other.

"I wondered a lot if I could handle all the moves and changes [that come with seminary]," said Suzy Brakhage. Suzy was new to the Lutheran Church-Missouri Synod when she married her husband, Joshua. He had left a career as a television newsman to pursue seminary.

"I know now that the moves and changes are not all bad," Suzy said. "Dealing with change allows you to grow in ways that you never thought possible."

Seminary made Suzy and her husband more resilient as a couple because they had to rely on each other through so many transitions. The same was true with Bryan and me. Our marriage has been a timeline of trading places, each of us supporting the other through major life ambitions to see our whole family through.

When you come to seminary for the first time, you have more questions than answers. Fear and uncertainty threaten to rule your world, because there is so much that you simply don't know about this vigorous process of becoming a pastor. When you return to seminary after vicarage, you can, for a short while, rest in somewhat of a familiar place. This isn't home, but it isn't foreign, either. More questions dance on the horizon, but there is a new energy about you and what the year ahead brings. Rest in the confidence that God has brought you this far, and He is continuing to work out His grand plan.

CHAPTER 12

Identity in the Call Process

"I believe that I shall look upon the goodness of
the Lord in the land of the living! Wait for the
Lord; be strong, and let your heart take courage;
wait for the Lord!"

-Psalm 27:13-14

During a women's class on transition early in our fourth year
at the seminary, each of us was asked to write three expectations
we have of the year ahead. I wrote:

- I expect this fourth year of seminary will be emotional,
  and that those emotional moments will at times arise
  without warning.
- I expect we will talk to our kids about the challenges and
  adventures of moving more than once.
- I expect that goodbyes from St. Louis will be hard.

I was right, on all accounts. As my husband moved into
his final year of seminary, I felt like I was in a strange comfort
zone. Finally, I was accustomed to this seminary life and had
developed close relationships with other women at the seminary.

I was accustomed to my husband's workload and sending him to the basement after dinner to toil away at homework. But time did not slow down. If anything, it sped up. As the months flew by, the awareness grew all the more palpable that soon we would be leaving this place and this lifestyle. Even as we had pulled through the transition between vicarage and year four of seminary, another big transition loomed.

Finally, the end was in sight. It was absolutely exciting. And absolutely terrifying.

Fourth year is a time of pondering tons of possibilities. The what-ifs are never ending. What if God gives us exactly what we want? What if He doesn't? What do we want, exactly? What do we not want? Does what we want matter when, at the end of the day, God's will prevails?

How does God work in the Call process, anyway?

In a sweeping survey at the beginning of fourth year, you will be asked to indicate your preferences for a type and location of parish. For most questions, you'll be asked to select one of three options on a scale of very open to not open at all. For example, how open are you to living in a parsonage? How open are you to a dual call setting, in a rural area? How open are you to contemporary worship? The placement director takes these surveys into consideration as calls come into his office, and uses the surveys, churches' particular needs and prayer to discern possible connections.

The call process is divinely directed, yet as is so common, God uses humans to go about His divinely directed work.

In our early meetings with the Placement Office, Dr. David Peter, Assistant to the Placement Director at Concordia Seminary, encouraged us – men and women alike – to cultivate a sense of wonder through the call process.

"It looks like a very human process, and it is," Peter told a group of about forty students and wives in the campus auditorium the fall of our fourth year.

Yet he also advised us to take the time and the space to observe the Holy Spirit's work.

"I assure you, He is involved," Peter told us. "He is the main mover."

Leslie Barron remembers wrestling over the tension between her desires – where she would love for her husband to be called – and God's will. A government contractor with an East Coast flare, she imagined how her life might be very different if her husband was sent to a place entirely unfamiliar to her. If God called them to Montana, for example, maybe she would forget her top-secret government security clearance and open a bakery, a dream that teased at her. She frequently needled the placement director in good humor: "As long as you don't send us to a cornfield in Iowa, we'll be fine," she liked to tell him.

All along, Bryan and I, like many others, had said we were "open" to wherever God would call us. But as the call process got underway, I started to think about that more critically. Did being "open" to where God wanted us mean ignoring the desires that were indeed within our hearts? Or were those desires from God Himself, a way of aligning us with His actual plan?

Tucked into the front cover of my journal is a folded map of the United States. I printed out that map in a flurry of thought one morning during our fourth year, following a restless night. All night long my mind had chattered: *Could you be happy in Mississippi? What about New Mexico, even if it doesn't snow? What if you get called to California?*

I printed a blank map of the United States the next morning. I had no idea how the fourth year Call process even worked then, as it was early on in the year, but I didn't care. I raided my son's crayon bucket for a blue crayon, and I started coloring. I wanted a visual to carry with me, something concrete to answer that question we had been asked and considered a thousand times: If you could live anywhere, where would it be?

As it turned out, that blue crayon revealed a lot. The area of the country where I most desired to live was a lot smaller on paper than it had appeared in my restless head. I had colored maybe one-fifth of the country. That map also helped me to get specific, to drill down into some details. Instead of coloring the whole state of Idaho, for example, I colored in only the eastern half (the half closest to my parents in Wyoming). Instead of coloring the whole state of Kansas, I had only shaded in the state's northeast corner. It was also through this coloring exercise that I realized the northern half of the United States was where I really wanted to be. My "ideal" was a place where winter came and stayed for a while. Growing up in Wyoming, I had experienced fierce winters that made spring an earnest and jubilant welcome. We felt we had earned that warm weather when it finally blossomed each year. I wanted that.

So when it came right down to it, although in theory we wanted to be open to wherever God called us, Bryan and I had specific desires for how and where we wanted to be involved in ministry. With the help of that blank map and my son's blue crayon, I could confidently answer where would be my ideal place to live. But was this the question God was asking, or was it a human question, defined by selfish desires and our own limited understanding? Were these desires mine alone, or were they longings God had placed within me?

I wanted to be that empty vessel, following with abandon wherever the Lord would lead. Yet deep down, I knew it would be a whole lot easier to follow if I *liked* where we were going. Could I remain wholly open if Bryan received a call to a part of the country with which I had no connection and, therefore, no interest in living? God does not promise us joy all of our days. In fact, He promises we will have trials and afflictions. How strong was I, really?

On the back of the map, I wrote in all caps: ANYWHERE CAN BE HOME AS LONG AS WE'RE TOGETHER. That map remains neatly folded inside the front cover of my journal, a reminder of the intense time of discerning leading up to the Call process.

For this season of life, you're waiting for a lot of things to fall into place. And that waiting is a strange thing. Because life continues. Still you make your weekly grocery list. Still you drop your kids off at school every day. Still you thaw meat for dinner.

It's a strange sensation, to go about the mundane tasks of life even as you're counting down the days to Call Day and such a big life moment. Meanwhile, time – that plain, apathetic, persistent force – marches on.

In her final year at the Sem, Kelsey Fink meditated on the ordinary tasks of life through a book called The Quotidian Mysteries: Laundry, Liturgies and Women's Work, by Kathleen Norris. The Quotidian Mysteries showed Kelsey parallels between life and liturgy; that life, like liturgy, can be quite ordinary, even as you await the grander moments.

Don't take these ordinary tasks for granted as you anticipate Call Day. In the Small Catechism, Luther refers to the more mundane tasks of life as "holy orders."[53] Kelsey faithfully continued her work of raising her children and taking care of things at home. As the days ticked away, she remembers thinking repeatedly, *I am here. It might only be for a year, but that doesn't mean God is not working. It does not mean He is not here.*

Rachel Geraci cared for her infant and worked part-time as a Mission and Ministry Director for Lutherans for Life. Her husband's fourth year at seminary was her first year on campus. At first, she didn't want to put effort toward making friends at the seminary, knowing she would only be there for a year. But soon enough she realized that God had put her on campus at a specific time for a specific period of time. Ignoring opportunities to

---

[53] See "Table of Duties," "Certain passages of scripture for various holy orders and positions, admonishing them about their duties and responsibilities," accessed May 4, 2020, http://bookofconcord.org/smallcatechism.php.

participate in community there was probably not God's intention for her.

Yet because of His mysteries and the often-subtle ways God works, it is admittedly easy to feel lost and confused – even lacking a purpose – as your days at the seminary wind down. By now you'll know well that it's easy to be discontent when you feel like you're not settled. Krista Weeks admitted to feeling stuck, both professionally and personally, as her husband, Kyle, finished out his seminary education.

"My jobs here are not my passion," she said. "I'm just trying to get us through school … I've been trying to rest in, 'This is where God has me. There's a reason why I'm here and why I'm here in this moment,'" she said.

Melissa Zech continued to be puzzled over the place of women's identities at seminary.

"I feel like there's so much more of me than ever gets to come out here," she said.

She knows God has called her to be a faithful daughter, friend, mother, and wife. Yet, at the seminary, she found herself without a home she could call her own. That detail threatened to shake her confidence in her God-given roles. Here she was, a homemaker without a house.

As my husband's fourth year cruised along, I began to notice changes in the tenors of conversations I was having and my own reluctance to initiate get-togethers with friends. I repeatedly put off checking in with Sara, my teacher friend, thinking she might want to start loosening our ties. By not checking in with her, I thought I was protecting her to the extent I could from a painful goodbye in the spring. But looking back, I think I was actually protecting myself. I didn't want to have to say goodbye. If I distanced myself little by little, then maybe our final goodbye would not be so hard.

Yet even as I resisted checking in with her, I longed for her to check in with me. During my family's four years at seminary,

Sara and I often met at Applebee's on a weeknight to catch up and simply hang out. I waited for a message or phone call from her, saying it was time to hang out again. But that message never came. Could it be that she was pulling away from me, too?

I was also sensitive to the friendships our boys had cultivated. More and more, it seemed like we were the ones initiating play dates and sleepovers; rarely were our boys invited by their friends to come over. Was that actually the case, or was I being hyper-sensitive?

Weirdly, the Call process is both a time of embracing and of letting go. You are embracing new possibilities and a major life change with your family. At the same time, you are letting go of another temporary life stage – the seminary years.

"It wasn't until our final year that I quit trying to speed up time," said Liz Garcia.

Through seminary life, Gretchen McGinley said she gained a sisterhood – a group of women who will always understand what seminary is like.

During my husband's fourth year, a dear friend and fellow seminary wife asked me if I was sad that I would soon be leaving my friends at seminary.

My answer was easy and immediate: "No."

I wasn't sad, for the very reason Gretchen pointed out: I had gained a sisterhood. I knew I would hardly ever see my seminary friends again, but I also knew we shared a bond that no one else had: we knew what life at seminary was like. We had met each other on the same journey – faithfully following our husbands on their path toward ministry – and we had suffered and thrived, cried and rejoiced, struggled and triumphed together along the way.

So many of the challenges that women specifically experience at seminary are universal. Through the relationships we had formed and the experiences we had shared, we grew together through that journey. No future friendship or experience would change that.

The intensive survey I mentioned earlier is the first major step of the Call Process. It happens early in your husband's fourth year. Then, you wait. You pray. You wait and you pray.

As the placement director and assistant director explain in regular meetings with fourth year students and their wives, interviews are only scheduled with congregations pursuing a team ministry scenario. One of the main reasons for the interview is to give the pastor who is currently installed at the church-in-question an opportunity to meet pastoral candidates whose survey responses closely align with the position the church is seeking to fill. The interviewee, in turn, gets a feel for the pastor and the church to determine if his gifts would fit well in that particular church and church leadership setting. Following each interview, both the interview committee and the pastoral candidate submit feedback about the interview to the placement director. The pastoral candidate is asked to indicate to the placement director whether he is open to receiving a Call to that specific church.

If your husband indicates he is open to a sole pastor position serving one or more parishes,[54] but is not open to a team ministry position, he will likely not receive any interview requests. Rather, he will simply be placed according to his survey response, a church's need and prayer.

I think it's fair to say that none of us are immune to the temptation to want to control where or to what congregations our husbands are called. Linda Nehring put it this way:

"Even though I would very much like to 'control' where we end up, I know at the same time that God has a better handle on this than I do and will put us where He wants … God puts you *where* He wants you *when* He wants you."

The interview process can be fun and exciting. It can also be riddled with angst.

---

[54] Positions as sole pastor often encompass dual parishes, or sometimes, three parishes, especially in rural settings.

My husband had three interview opportunities with churches that by and large fit what we were looking for in a church home. Two of those interviews were scheduled for the middle of a weekday and were in-person interviews. One of them – the church to where we most strongly hoped he would be called – was scheduled for an evening via Skype. If we were to rank his interview performance across the three interviews (and we did), his worst interview was with the church to which he most longed to be called. Following the interviews, Bryan indicated to the placement director that he preferred not to be called to two of the three churches. He indicated he strongly preferred to be called to one.

In the weeks that followed, I watched my husband wrestle with very real doubts and fears. So convinced was he that he would not be called to the church he most wanted that he had to squarely question whose will was more important: his or God's. He knew the right answer, of course, but knowing the answer and fully walking in it are two different things. His desire to serve at a specific church overshadowed the larger and more important question of where God wanted him. His greatest challenge in that time was surrendering his own longings to God's will. He had to trust that God would work through him, even if that meant walking down a road he didn't necessarily want to be on.

I wrestled with my own share of disappointment in that time. We had lived in this "what-if" zone for three-and-a-half years. Together, we had talked through possibilities. What if he was called here? What if he were called there? We knew going down this road of seminary and into the ministry would require heaps of faith and trust. In this huge and lingering moment of uncertainty, why couldn't my husband be stronger – stronger for God and stronger for our family?

Luke 5:1-11 tells the story of the fish in the net. The disciples had been out on the Sea of Galilee all night with nary a fish to show for it. Jesus stepped into Peter's boat, and after teaching the people from there, told Peter to "Put out into deep water, and let down the nets for a catch" (verse 4). Peter responded in faith. But when the nets filled up with so many fish that they began to break and the boats began to sink, how did Peter respond? He responded in fear: "Go away from me, Lord; I am a sinful man!"[55]

Why did Peter respond this way?

Peter responded in fear for the same reason my husband seemingly lacked strength when it he needed it most: the nearer you draw to Jesus, the more you feel your own sinfulness and unworthiness.

Through the rocky time of waiting, I prayed that my husband would feel God's peace and strength. I prayed that God would raise him up onto firm ground and help him stand as an unshakable, devoted servant-leader I believed God was shaping him to be. At the same time, I knew my husband was human – his pursuit to become a pastor did not make him immune to doubt and fear.

Kyla Rodriguez prayed Psalm 16 through the interview process.

> Keep me safe, my God,
>   for in you I take refuge.
> I say to the Lord, "You are my Lord;
>   apart from you I have no good thing."
> I say of the holy people who are in the land,
>   "They are the noble ones in whom is all my delight."
>   Those who run after other gods will suffer more and more.
>   I will not pour out libations of blood to such gods
>   or take up their names on my lips.
> Lord, you alone are my portion and my cup;
>   you make my lot secure.

---

[55] Luke 5:8

The boundary lines have fallen for me in
pleasant places;
  surely I have a delightful inheritance.
I will praise the Lord, who counsels me;
  even at night my heart instructs me.
I keep my eyes always on the Lord.
  With him at my right hand, I will not be shaken.
Therefore my heart is glad and my tongue rejoices;
  my body also will rest secure,
because you will not abandon me to the realm of
the dead,
  nor will you let your faithful one see decay.
You make known to me the path of life;
  you will fill me with joy in your presence,
with eternal pleasures at your right hand.

As vocations come and go, we must trust God to help us work into the new identities to which He calls us. Even though so much uncertainty – where you'll end up or what your life will look like after Call – surrounds you, hold on to your one vocation that will never change: you are a baptized child of God.

Juli Lamie meditated on this truth in her husband's final year at the seminary. A young mother of one who dreamed of raising a large family, Juli wrestled with the uncertainties that came with the "what-if" questions. What if she was not able to have more children? What if her roles changed through the years? It's true that once you're a parent, you're always a parent. But even children grow up. Then what?

Through continued reflection, Juli realized that almost every vocation has a season. As she began to see herself first as a child of God and second, as everything else, she realized those what-if questions didn't matter nearly as much.

"Being a child of God makes me valuable. It makes me significant. It makes me secure," she said.

The week before Call Day, Rachel Warner read a chapter about identity in Susan Miller's book, <u>After the Boxes are Unpacked</u>. She was dating fourth-year student Daniel Warner and loved her hard-earned and well-established career as an architect at a St. Louis firm. Professor's wife Renee Gibbs had invited Rachel to join what has lovingly become known as "The Boxes" class for women on campus, and Rachel was glad to find a welcoming community of women who were asking the same questions she was – *Who am I in this process* and *where do I fit?* This chapter illustrated those very vocations that come and go. Later, she and Daniel ran into the placement director on campus. The placement director promised Daniel that he would be called to a small mountain town out west – exactly what Daniel was hoping for. Then, he looked at Rachel and said, "But I didn't get a chance to know you and I'm not sure there will be a job for you there."

Having just read the chapter on identity, Rachel knew she should be okay with that. But she panicked, nonetheless. Who she was had been wrapped up in the vocation of "architect" for so long. Who would she be if that role was stripped from her?

"My career is important," Rachel said, but in that moment, she knew that Daniel's vocation was more important.

She would have to train her brain to prioritize differently.

Staking your primary vocation on being a child of God – the spiritual vocation – changes everything. For Erica McCarty, this means leaning more on who God has created her to be and less on what she does.

You are, after all, a human *being*, not a human *doing*.

"To be" is the infinitive of "You are." What does God say about "you are?"

Just as the Call process is both a time of embracing and of letting go, it is also a time of both apprehension and excitement. The butterflies in your stomach are real. The ceremony and the people, all gathered for your family and other fourth year families, are real.

Apprehension noses its way in with fears and uncertainties about how you will be received at a new-to-you church. How are your actions going to affect or influence others' experiences in the ministry?

"It's not as simple as, 'Just be yourself 100 percent of the time,'" said Amy Will.

You might suddenly feel like you are not cut out to be a pastor's wife – that all of your flaws will be exposed and that (gulp) people might actually see that you're *human*.

"I am trying to be someone who acts out of love rather than selfishness, but I fail at this *all the time*," said Suzy Brakhage.

Do you really have what it takes to do this?

That question carries Satan's echoes from the Garden of Eden. *Did God really tell you ...?*

Kelsey Fink kept 2 Corinthians 12:9 close during the Call ceremony. "But he said to me, 'My grace is sufficient for you, for my power is made perfect in weakness.' Therefore I will boast all the more gladly about my weaknesses, so that Christ's power may rest on me."

In all circumstances, God's grace is sufficient. Christ is enough, and Christ is always enough.

As names are called and Calls are announced, tune into the joy and excitement that permeates the room. But be aware also of Call envy. Know that there is no perfect Call. Trust that God's hand is not only in it; His hand guides the whole process, for everyone – everyone! – involved.

Remember all of those what-ifs that tugged at you like energetic puppies throughout the past year? Ask yourself how God will use you. Where is He sending you? It is just the place He needs you, whether you can see it or not. Imagine being able to put nails into walls, because you'll be living somewhere long enough for that to make sense. Imagine exploring the grocery store in your new community and what new foods or regional favorites you might encounter. Imagine being invited into other peoples' lives and inviting other people into yours. Imagine doing life with a church family, *your* church family.

"I'm excited to see how God is going to meet our needs," said Kim Bartok.

"I'm excited to get a new place, to start over, in a way," said Krista Weeks. "I'm so interested to know where God sees us working in this country, and in this ministry."

It's no secret: the Call process is not easy. God will challenge you. He will ask you to fully trust Him. And fully trusting Him may mean taking one or more steps in the dark. But know that, if He has called you to it, He won't leave you hanging. The focus, in the Call process and in every area of your future ministry, is not what you are doing, but what He is doing through you. God is bigger than you. Let that be an encouragement for you on Call Day!

Consider the comfort in Jude's benediction: "To him who is able to keep you from stumbling and to present you before his glorious presence without fault and with great joy—to the only God our Savior be glory, majesty, power and authority, through Jesus Christ our Lord, before all ages, now and forevermore! Amen!"

PART 4

Transition from the Call to the Church

CHAPTER 13

Wrestling with God AFTER the Call

"He performs wonders that cannot be fathomed,
miracles that cannot be counted."

-Job 9:10

Call Day at the seminary comes and goes in a flurry. The nerves and excitement rise up like a tidal wave. The moment arrives: your husband receives the direction for which you've waited so long.

Finally, you know where you're going.

The news is official, and it is public.

In a way, Call Day is like a wedding. Emotions are high and the sense of anticipation is palpable. After what seems like an eternity of waiting, the big day arrives. You are surrounded by family and your treasured friends from the seminary. There is pomp and circumstance – way more to the ceremony than that simple declaration you've been envisioning for so long. God is front and center. You wait. You take a deep breath. You try to stay focused on the message. All the while, the big moment lingers.

And then, it comes. Everyone cheers. The declaration is official.

Emotions wash over you. You want to cherish the excitement and bottle up the positive energy. You never want to forget this moment.

As I sat with my two boys, my parents and my husband's parents in a packed pew in a packed chapel at Concordia Seminary the night of the Call ceremony, I didn't realize (or, at least I wasn't thinking about) the multitude of friends and acquaintances who were tuning into the livestream of the service from across the country. When my husband's placement was announced – Zion Lutheran Church in Rapid City, South Dakota – my phone began to ping with messages of encouragement and excitement.

People everywhere were cheering us on. The church itself had organized a watch party, and members of the congregation gathered at the church to watch the ceremony together.

This was a shared moment. It didn't belong only to our family; it belonged to everyone who cared about and had invested in us and in this journey.

You want to live in this moment. And you do.

Some families will not be surprised at all to learn where the husband's first Call is. Others will reel in shock. Some will be apprehensive. Others will glow with excitement.

But time marches on. Tomorrow is still another day. Call Day is a culminating moment. But seminary is not over. Your husband still has two weeks of classes to complete. He still has papers to write, books to read, academic work to finish.

Meanwhile, you have work to do. And now, you have a million questions to go along with that work. You will find yourself figuring out how to close out this chapter of your life while you're still living it. Your husband's role is soon to take on a whole new meaning. Changes are coming at you from all directions. Just like that, you're saying goodbye to people you've shared pieces of your life with for the past four years. You have decisions to make, details to keep track of and dates to schedule. You'll have a move to coordinate. It might be a move of sixty miles, or it might be a move of two-thousand-sixty miles. A house-hunting trip will be on your horizon, if the church to where your husband was called does not have a parsonage. You'll have a new congregation to meet and a new community to get to know. You may have to re-define some family roles. It's a wonderfully exciting time. And it's exhausting.

As Liz Garcia looks back at that transition, she remembers the exhaustion. "There is so much to figure out with housing and meeting everyone for the first time," she said, not to mention getting the family settled into a "new" normal.

It seems counter-intuitive, but this is a time to give yourself extra rest (if you can), extra time for reflection and extra grace.

Because change (and this change might just be with a capital "C") can threaten the core of who we are.

"I feel like every time I move, I struggle with who I am," said Jamie DiLiberto.

What makes you who you are? Your life's roles certainly do – a wife, a mother, an employee, a professional, a friend. But so do your surroundings. If you have lived in an apartment on campus, what will your life look like away from that close-knit community? If you have rented a home, what memories will you take with you from that place? What has life at seminary taught you about who you are – and who you are not?

While life at the seminary looks different for everyone, the community aspect is largely uniform. You come, knowing you'll be there temporarily. You come, knowing your husband has some hard years of studies ahead of him. The seminary campus is a shared space where together we experience the ups and downs of life preparing for ministry in the public sphere.

But as you embark on your husband's first Call, your journey will look different than anyone else who is going out into the mission field. Some men will receive Calls to large suburban churches with a Senior Pastor. Others will go into a rural setting as a sole pastor. Some congregations will be vibrant; others will be struggling. You should have a fairly clear idea of the particular ministry situation you're headed to based on the thoroughly prepared paperwork you receive on Call Day. But there are still a lot of unknowns ahead.

Even though each of our journeys will be different, as we prepare to leave seminary, we all have this in common: there is no easy way to uproot a life, uproot a family, pack your life into boxes, land somewhere new.

Our final few days at the seminary were typical of those of most outgoing seminary families we knew. We taped up the final moving boxes. Our hearts pounded at the thought that our whole lives sat inside of the fifty-six-foot moving truck parked outside our door. We mopped our dirt off the floors, washed our dirt off the walls. Our two vehicles were packed floor-to-ceiling with everything we could imagine we'd need for the coming three-to-four weeks, cleaning supplies that the moving company wouldn't pack and four plants that I adored.

One sentence stands out among many in my journal from this fast-paced, chaotic time: "The changes keep coming, and they won't slow down for a while."

The morning we were scheduled to leave St. Louis, my husband, our two boys and I stood in a circle in our empty kitchen, holding hands. We prayed for the home we were leaving and for the new owners. We thanked God for the tremendous blessings our house had showered on us during the seminary season. We prayed for our new home in Rapid City and the many hours and details that would be required to get there.

It's difficult to talk about the house hunting experience that follows Call, because that experience looks completely different for everyone. Adam and Julie Bridgman rented an apartment in Janesville, Wisconsin, sight unseen, two weeks after Call Day. Jim and Kim Bartok spent one day house hunting in Ozark, Missouri, with their three young children the week after Call, but found no houses that would work. Kim's mom, who had joined them at a timeshare in the Ozarks, stuck around for an extra day, to explore the town and be there in case anything else came on the market. Two more houses came on the market while she was there, but one was way out of their price range and the other was too small and in poor condition.

Kim's mom, however, was unflinchingly convinced that God would provide her daughter and family a home. She told the realtor that she looked forward to receiving his phone call later that day, telling her another house had come on the market that was perfect for Kim and her family.

That house came on the market a few hours later.

"It was the perfect house, the perfect set-up," Kim said. "We bought the house without seeing it and yes, it is perfect for us."

The week after Call Day, my husband and I had leaned wholly on grandparents to stay with our boys in St. Louis while he and I flew to South Dakota for a week of house hunting. The housing market was hot – great for us as sellers in St. Louis, but not great for us as buyers in Rapid City. Houses were selling fast and high. After looking at 11 houses in one day, we made an offer on one that fit our needs, not because we absolutely loved it, but because we were afraid that if we didn't make an offer, it would be gone the next day. With a definitive timeframe for our house hunting, it was essential that we find a place to live. There was no "let's wait and see." We had to act, and act we did.

During this time, God worked on my humility and demanded my trust. Like most people, I imagined what a "dream home" might look like. Truth be told, I had been building a dream home in my mind for the better part of fifteen years. The time was never right to chase that dream. Bryan's work as an engineer in the years before seminary had meant a life of packing up and moving every eighteen-to-twenty-four-months for us. seminary, of course, was one more temporary landing place. With so many moves under our belts, both Bryan and I prayed that this major move from St. Louis to Rapid City would be our last. I prayed that we would find a home that we loved, where we could settle down with our family.

It seemed that God wanted to use this time to challenge my attachment to material desires. How important is a dream home to you? He seemed to be asking, as house after house that we looked at lacked the appeal I had so imagined. Do you trust Me to take care of you?

Throughout our house-hunting journey and even through the signing of the paperwork, I fell on the faith I had so thoroughly contemplated at the seminary: God lights our way, but so often He only provides enough light for us to see the step directly in front of us. The step directly in front of me was the paperwork to own a home I did not love but that would be more than sufficient for my family during this next season. Still, God was not opening the door to my dream home. He may never. But in that time of discerning, I had to ask what was more important: scoring my dream home because I had waited for it for so long, or seizing the moment to secure what we needed while trusting that God was in control. The choice was obvious: "Many are the plans in a person's heart, but it is the Lord's purpose that prevails" (Proverbs 19:21).

In the months and weeks leading up to Call Day, my anxiety swelled as the realization grew stronger that I could not protect my kids from an impending major move.

Our six-year-old piped up from the backseat: "Do we have to move?"

"Yes," his nine-year-old brother said matter-of-factly, beating me to a response.

This question, in some shape or form, was coming out more often from our kids, and almost always, it showed up without warning. We never wanted to take their questions lightly, and we knew it was important to stay positive with them.

At the same time, we didn't want to sugarcoat the truth: yes, we would be leaving, and yes, it would be hard.

Our oldest son fell apart on the night of his last day of school in St. Louis. First, he cried quietly, pressed against the wall on the far side of his bed. I felt his cold, wet cheek, and told him it was okay to cry. He sidled up next to me and let it come. He cried and cried. I cried with him, torn between being strong for him and being weak with him. I had no words. Nothing I could think of to say seemed like the right thing. I couldn't tell him I knew what leaving third grade friends and an entire elementary school felt like; I didn't know. I couldn't tell him this was no big deal; it was.

In all honesty, I couldn't imagine a cross-country move from his young and unassuming perspective. Could he or his brother possibly know the deeper ramifications of a major move, that saying goodbye to their friends and teachers and school and baseball teams and all that was familiar was so much more than a simple, "See you tomorrow?" Could they possibly know to what extent we were about to pull the rug out from under them?

When I was growing up, I always felt sorry for the new kids in school – and relief that I was not one of them. Our boys would soon be those very kids I once pitied. We were asking a lot of them. And if I were honest, I questioned sometimes whether I would be strong enough to support my kids through that tremendous process of uprooting and settling down somewhere else. I prayed fervently that God would use the entire seminary experience, from the past four years to the days and weeks to come, to help mold our boys into the strong Christian men He desires them to be.

As I lay with my son on his bed, I could assure him that our family was in this tremendous transition together and that, no matter what else changed, our family unit would not. We would continue to love each other and support each other and stay together, all of us, through it. God's love for us would not change.

Liz Garcia recognized the silver lining along with the challenge of uprooting kids.

"I believe my kids are better for our years at the seminary, but the transitions were still hard on them," she said.

At a women's retreat during our last year of seminary, pastor's wife and writer Heidi Goehmann reminded us through a Bible study that none of us is a child without a home.

We belong to God.

In the overwhelm of this transition period, no matter who we are or how old, it is so easy to get swept away in a sea of chaos and uncertainty. How easy it is to forget or drown out the most foundational of all identities: child of God.

You are a loved child of God.

You are a forgiven child of God.

Especially in times of uncertainty, we need to remind each other of this truth, and we need to remind our kids of it, too.

"With every transition, when you feel like you're left with nothing all over again, you remind yourself that you're a baptized child of God," said Kelsey Fink. "Coming back to that again and again is always the best place to be."

It doesn't matter how many times you start over. The emotions are there, and they are real. As you find yourself navigating this new season of life, you should expect frustration. You should expect isolation. You may well encounter moments of pure fear, feeling like you're dangling on a limb that is about to snap. You may be so caught up in all of the changes, the newness and the ever-growing to-do list that you feel spiritually starved.

But God promises He will never leave you nor forsake you. Cling to that promise. Having your heart in multiple places is hard and beautiful.

Cling to that promise when you fear. Cling to that promise when you doubt. Cling to that promise when you can't see what lies ahead.

There were times in our new state of South Dakota that I felt downright dumb. I did not understand a tax notice we received in the mail. It was not like any of the notices I had seen before in other states we had lived in. How was it that, at age thirty six, I still could not completely understand a property tax bill and how property taxes worked?

That mean voice was silenced by a gentler, more logical one. Every state operates differently. Could it be the reason I did not understand the property tax bill in South Dakota was because we had never lived in South Dakota?

I knew I needed to give myself extra grace.

Transition demands patience of us, and extra kindness to ourselves and to our loved ones.

But just as starting over brings big challenges, you should also expect it to bring joy and excitement. There are big advantages to starting over again and again. The many transitions of seminary can be tremendous confidence boosters. Because I've had to do it so many times, I can unequivocally say I am confident driving/navigating new places, walking into a church for the first time and meeting/introducing myself to new people.

Perhaps the biggest blessing to starting over so many times is that I have friends in a lot of places. This makes planning vacations and even miniature getaways extra fun. Long-time pastor's wife Beth DeMeritt happily claims that she prays for friends in all of the thirteen places her family has lived. There are good people everywhere.

Ecclesiastes 3:1 tells us there is a season for everything. There is "a time to plant and a time to uproot" (verse 2). God ordained seasons in part to give us the gift of newness.

When her family moved to Boca Raton, Florida, for her husband's first Call, Nikki Kubowicz shared in a Facebook post with the women still at the seminary: "My hope for this coming year is to enjoy all the newness this year brings."

There's something refreshing about constant newness.

One thing you have at your disposal as a new pastor's family in a new town is an entire community of people who can't wait to meet you. You also have in that community a network of knowledge. I couldn't wait to tap into that network when we moved to Rapid City. When our vehicle needed an oil change, we would simply ask members of the congregation where they went for oil changes. When we wanted a nice evening out, we would ask the congregation members what their favorite restaurants in town were. When we wanted to explore local stomping grounds on a free weekend, we'd ask people from church where we should go.

But what about more personal services, like a doctor, a dentist, a counselor or even a hairstylist? I hesitated to reach out for recommendations there. Of course, we had doctors and dentists, counselors and hairstylists in our congregation. Of course, it would be easy to call their offices and set up appointments as a new patient or a new client. On one hand, utilizing a member of the congregation for these services seemed like a no-brainer; already there was a level of trust established, as we were both Christian and belonged to the same church. But belonging to the same church is what made me hesitate. Did I really want a congregation member to know personal things about me, such as my weight and my blood pressure and my history with birth control? What about my family's history of depression – and my own decade-long struggle with anxiety?

Many pastors' wives recognize the tension in these decisions. You want to be open and genuine with people. You want to show them that you, too, are human. But you also don't want to put your flaws on display for people who look up to your husband and who are, by default, watching you.

There are, of course, no set-in-stone expectations for how to handle these kinds of things as a pastor's wife. At the end of the day, you must do what you are comfortable with. Some women have no problem having their teeth cleaned by a member of the congregation. Some women will put on a hospital gown and step on a scale in front of a congregation member without a second thought. Some women avoid mixing their personal and self-care needs with the church all together. There is no wrong or right way to pursue services like this.

As a pastor's wife, you are or will be the wearer of many hats. You want to take care of yourself in the best ways you know how so that you are ready and eager to serve your congregation with joy and love, and so that you model good care of the temple God has provided you.

The truth is, God never stopped working on us as women through the seminary years. Just as He worked in your husband to prepare him to become a pastor, He worked in you to become a pastor's wife. As you find yourself navigating new roles and new surroundings, trust that the newness is part of His grand plan. Even Luther, in the sixteenth century, recognized that vocations can and do change according to time and circumstances.[56]

As you find yourself in a new community, in a new parish and in a new role, I hope you wonder with excitement how you are going to fit into the ministry life, and where your gifts and talents can be best used. But I also hope that the past months and years of transition have given you a stronger – not weaker – sense of identity, of who Christ is calling you to be. What are your gifts? What are your strengths? What are your weaknesses?

During our vicarage year, a member of the church asked me if I would be interested in joining the choir. Singing is not my strength, nor is it something I am particularly passionate about. Because I knew this about myself, it was easy to turn down that invitation. When the music director invited me to play flute, however, I agreed without a second thought.

As you find yourself in a new place, don't try to be someone you're not. But be open to trying new things and to stretching yourself in new areas, guided by prayer.

---

[56] Robert Kolb and Charles P. Arand, *The Genius of Luther's Theology: A Wittenburg Way of Thinking for the Contemporary Church* (Baker Academic, 2008), 64.

"Because of the Lord's great love we are not consumed, for his compassions never fail. They are new every morning; great is your faithfulness. I say to myself, 'The Lord is my portion; therefore I will wait for him. The Lord is good to those whose hope is in him, to the one who seeks him; it is good to wait quietly for the salvation of the Lord" (Lamentations 3:22-26).

CHAPTER 14

Community in the Church

As women, most of us thrive on relationships. We need people, and we need people to need us. But navigating relationships in the church and in the community where your husband serves is not an easy thing for a lot of women. You want to be open. You want to be authentic. Yet, because you're the wife of a pastor, how candid can you really be with people – especially members of your congregation?

"That's been a burning question for me the whole time," said Kelsey Fink prior to her husband receiving a Call. "That type of guarded life scares me."

According to a 2017 LifeWay Research study,[57] sixty-nine percent of pastors' wives feel they have few people they can confide in.

As a pastor's wife, Rachel Warner knows she has to be careful about being too vulnerable with people in the church. Partially because of that, finding good friends has proved difficult for her.

Erica McCarty can relate.

---

[57] "Pastor's Spouses Experience Mixed Blessings," LifeWay Research, September 12, 2017, https://lifewayresearch.com/2017/09/12/pastors-spouses-experience-mixed-blessings/. The survey takes into consideration responses of 720 pastors' spouses across Protestant church denominations.

"I am careful about friendships I build in the church because of my husband's role," she said. "It can be difficult to be real with a person whose husband is their church leader."

As pastors' wives who are new to the role, new to the church and likely new to our geographical surroundings, how do we interact with people in the congregation? Where do we find friends?

When my family moved to Rapid City, I came to know 100-plus people on a first-name basis quickly. I love getting to know people and hearing their stories, so at face value, this was exciting for me.

In short, this is your ministry to the church: you do life with people. You share in the joys and sorrow of life with a bigger purpose in mind. And you ultimately see lives and families changed.

As I shook hands in the receiving line following my husband's ordination and installation, I wanted to see these people as Jesus saw them: blameless, without baggage or agendas. Standing in the back of the church after the ceremony, I was confident and energetic. Bryan and I were greeting the congregation members as strangers, yet as brothers and sisters in Christ. Already, I longed for a history with these people: I wanted to know their excitements and their hurts, their strengths and their weaknesses.

God puts people in our path to grieve the painful moments and celebrate the best moments. Who in this congregation would we do life with? Who would we celebrate with, and who would we grieve with? What experiences lay ahead that our family and these families would share?

Anna Davis felt especially cared for in her church when her husband was gone on a mission trip for three weeks. Because the whole congregation knew he was gone, the congregation also knew that Anna was on her own for three weeks with their three kids.

"That meant that I received support and blessings from some unexpected places," Anna said.

If her husband had a different job, not as many people would have been aware that he was gone.

As a pastor's wife, one of your most important roles is to get to know your congregation, both as a whole and in its parts. One of my first goals as a pastor's wife was to introduce myself to one person or one family every week. To be honest, that took a lot of forethought and energy on my part. It's not as easy as it sounds! Introducing yourself means accepting certain risks. You might be perceived as overly assertive. You might catch someone on a bad day. You might call someone Martha, only to remember an hour later (to your horror) that the woman you so cheerfully called out to is actually named Betty. Give yourself grace (like Jesus does) and practice the eighth commandment: always think of someone in the best light.

I admit, as a relatively new pastor's wife, all of this is still new to me. The bright-shiny newness may have worn off (the "honeymoon" phase), but I still have a lot to learn. I know it is crucial to spend time with people in the congregation. But I haven't done that enough.

Seasoned pastor's wife Kyra Wurm shared with me that making friends in the church early on was harder than she thought it would be, and she is a strong extrovert. Yet she also had not completely embraced her identity or role as "Pastor's wife." Her reluctance to take on that role influenced her opportunities for relationships in the church. It took a lot of time for her to grow comfortable with her new identity and to learn to embrace the good and the bad that come with it.

Liz Garcia found that many people in her congregation did not feel comfortable introducing themselves to her. Meeting people can be awkward, and most people don't have a need to practice it very often. Liz recognized that the many transitions built into her husband becoming a pastor gave her plenty of opportunities to practice introducing herself in new situations. So even when others didn't initiate, Liz focused her energy on introducing herself to others and letting people see that she was nice – and normal, like them.

Michelle Knauss connected with members of her congregation by attending events that were a part of their lives – baseball games, birthday parties and other social gatherings. Her family and other families in the congregation have helped each other with do-it-yourself projects around their homes. These congregation members are the ones the Knausses think of when they want to get together with others. Connecting with congregation members this way was a blessing that Michelle had not anticipated.

As you're getting to know people, realize that every church has a diverse population. All kinds of people make up a church congregation. We are called to share our lives with everyone whom God puts before us, and we are called to be kind to everyone. But we will inevitably share more of our lives with certain people in the congregation, simply because we have more things in common with them or are in a similar life stage. Just as Scripture tells us to love everyone, it also encourages us to practice discernment. Be wise with the people who you choose to share the more personal parts of your life with. And be wise with the people who choose to share the more personal parts of their lives with you. Because we are all sinners, it is important that we test all of our relationships against Scripture. Colossians 2:8 says, "See to it that no one takes you captive by philosophy and empty deceit, according to human tradition, according to the elemental spirits of the world, and not according to Christ." In Matthew 10:16, the Holy Spirit calls us to be wise as serpents and innocent as doves.

As the wife of the pastor, I am finding that there is a fine line between being open and authentic with people and keeping some aspects of my life and my husband's life private. I am still navigating that boundary line, and I probably always will be.

It didn't take long for me to realize that almost every single person I knew in our new community was a member of our church. I wanted to branch out. I wanted to meet people outside of the church, build relationships with others who were not connected to Zion. But how?

To be honest, many women feel at a loss when it comes to making friends as a pastor's wife. Whether it's the stigma of being a "pastor's wife" or family/work responsibilities that keep us from branching out, a lot of us just don't do it.

"My life just doesn't allow a lot of outside connection," said Liz Slavens.

Through the heavy transitions that seminary and life in pastoral ministry requires, Michelle Knauss said she has learned a lot about herself. She knows she needs time to feel settled and develop friendships — those things don't come naturally for her.

Rachel Warner found a community outside the walls of the church in a Zumba class.

"It's not kindred spirit kind of friends," she said, "but it's nice to have some regularity and familiarity."

Liz Garcia eventually met the mother of a Kindergartner who was in her daughter's class at the church's school. The mother was not a church member, and, like Liz, she was new in town. As they got to know each other, Liz felt free to be more open with her and connect on a different level than she felt she was able to connect with church members.

We know that God puts different people in our lives at different times for different reasons. We know that God's timing is bigger than ours, and that often it looks nothing like what would make sense to us. Leaning into this has helped me to more fully embrace opportunities for friendships and relationships. For example, when we moved to Rapid City, I connected with another mom whose child attends the same school as our kids. We learned we lived two blocks from each other, and one day, she invited me to walk the neighborhood with her once a week. I agreed, eager to make friends and meet people outside of the church.

Many women have made connections via community interest groups and library groups. Heidi Goehmann said she connects with people outside of the church by intentionally engaging at the public library in every new town she finds herself in.

"My number-one rule for friends is that they never ask me to be different than who I am and I will do the same," she said. "There's lots of God and Jesus talk in all my friendships because I don't know how to not talk about that part of my life. But I also have to be comfortable to hear ideas I may not agree with and honor them, while not incorporating them and being open about the fact that I see things differently."

Heidi's four suggestions for connecting are just as important in your new church as they were at the seminary:

1. Cry out to God
2. Walk up to one person
3. Be awkward and let others be awkward
4. Start the conversation

When Heidi's family moved to Nebraska for her husband's Call, Heidi started the conversation by walking her neighborhood with a basket of hot cocoa and tea packets. She knocked on her neighbors' doors and delivered the packets one-by-one, introducing herself to people as she went. It was awkward at times. The task demanded energy and intention. But Heidi did not wait for others to recognize that her family was the new family on the block. Nor did she wait for community to find her. Instead, equipped with God's grace and goodness, she stepped out, in courage and in faith.

God doesn't call us to look inward. He calls us to look outward and to trust Him.

If we can wholly trust in His purpose and His timing, no relationship is a waste of time.

But God also calls us to be patient. Though there is no hard data to prove or measure it, multiple pastor's wives have told me it may take three-to-four years to feel fully invested and connected with a church, a community and with the people you do life with. That's a hard pill to swallow; three-to-four years is a long time!

One of the biggest struggles for me as a new pastor's wife has been this very thing. I want fast friends, because I miss (how I miss!) the deep-rooted, longstanding friendships that our years at seminary gave me. I want good friends here, and I want them right now! Yet I know I can't hurry relationships. There are no shortcuts to establishing solid, trustworthy friends.

Making friends is not a fast process. Good friends take time!

I am grateful to have met many, many wonderful people in the months since we've moved to Rapid City. I would even say I've made many new friends and acquaintances. But on a deeper level, these early months in my role as a pastor's wife have been lonely. I miss the history that many people have with each other here. I want to fit right into that, but I know I can't. I can't magically produce a long-term relationship. At the end of the day, I have to fall back on Christ and His promise that He is with me. Time is that powerful force, guided and shaped by the Holy Spirit.

I am also finding that the sisterhood I gained at the seminary is crucial right now. My sisters in Christ are settling in to a new normal all over the country. As a new pastor's wife in Rapid City, I might be physically alone. But I have friends in other places who are in the same season I'm in. A recent phone call with a friend from seminary reminded me that I am not alone in my struggles and my questions. 'How are you settling in to your new home?' she wanted to know. 'Do you ever feel anxious or question how God is working?' 'Do you watch your budget to the penny?' As we verbalized our questions and our own experiences, I realized I am far from alone on this journey. We are wandering this wilderness together, my seminary sisters and I. Even though they are not geographically close, I take comfort in knowing I am not alone.

Who are those women for you? Reach out to them. They will be thrilled to hear from you. And chances are, you have been on their minds, too.

Another valuable resource during your first few years as the pastor's family in the church is PALS, or Post-seminary Applied Learning and Support. PALS is the official program of The Lutheran Church—Missouri Synod created to assist the new pastor and his wife in the transition from seminary to full time parish ministry. The program was created by the Council of Presidents and the Board for Pastoral Education in 1998. Trained facilitators (veteran pastors and their wives) chosen by district presidents facilitate and mentor new pastors and their wives and children through the first three years of the pastor's first call. PALS groups, available in most districts, meet up to six days a year. These gatherings include worship, topic study, casuistry, and fellowship. Each group chooses its own topics of study. Topics may include the pastor's family devotional life, teaching a Bible class, transitioning into an urban or rural setting, isolation and loneliness, how to handle conflict in the parish, boundaries and expectations of the pastor's wife, preaching-related topics, conducting a funeral or wedding, how to process a call, and many more. PALS offers you the chance to be a part of a community of people in your district who are at roughly the same point on the ministry journey as you are. PALS is one more place where you can find strength and encouragement from people who understand the complexities and unique blessings of life in ministry.

In your new normal, and in your new role as a pastor's wife, some people will love you. Others might appear to be stand-offish. How do you go about day-to-day life in this new place? Where do you even start?

Here are three thoughts:

1. **Observe.** Just as my experience during the whole of vicarage year was to observe what was taking place around me at the church, there is a definite season for this as your husband comes into a church as a new pastor. Observing is not only wise; it is respectful. It shows the congregation that you're paying attention, and that you care about the church and the ministries already in place. One of the worst yet strongest temptations for pastors and pastors' wives is to come roaring into a church, expecting to change or improve things. Choose to see yourself as an observer rather than a fixer. It's fine to think of yourself as a problem solver, but before you go about solving problems, take the time to identify what the problems are. At the same time, be sure to identify what the gifts are of your new congregation. Remember that your church community has likely been in existence for a long time. An idea that may be new to you may have already been done or tried. A solution you want to put forward may have already been suggested in years past. You will earn far more respect if you pay attention to others first, value their ideas and their efforts before putting your own ideas out there. Show the church you care by first getting to know the people and the ministries that make the church what it is.

2. **Be yourself.** Allow people to see you for who you really are. Admit your weaknesses. Serve with your strengths. Use your strengths and your weaknesses as rudders to guide you through relationship and volunteer opportunities. As the pastor's wife, you might feel like you are expected to say "yes" to every request for help that comes your way. But that is not God's expectation. He gives you strengths and weaknesses for a reason. Your strengths are someone

Seven Ways to Make Connections

1. **Find a community group focused on one of your core interests**: a photography group, a genealogy group, a book club. Search for groups via Facebook or Meetup.com, and keep your eyes out for flyers posted on community boards, in the library, and (if applicable) at your children's school. If you can't find a group centered around a particular hobby that interests you, don't be afraid to start one!

2. **Get to know parents of kids who participate in the same activities your kids participate in.** Diana Wallace connected with other parents of kids on a traveling baseball team. Nicole Knutson made friends through a ballet studio her children attend. Debbie Okubo still gets together with parents of her children's friends, years after the kids graduated high school.

3. **Reach out to fellow pastors' wives.** You can easily find pastors' wives in your LCMS district via the district's communications. PALS is also an excellent resource to connect to newer pastors' wives in your region. Join the LCMS Wives of Pastors Facebook group to connect with LCMS pastors' wives across the country. Many of

else's weaknesses. Your weaknesses are someone else's strengths. God depends on everyone in the congregation (not just you) to do the work of the church.

Just because you're a pastor's wife does not mean you must have a leader mentality. More than half of the women I interviewed for this book consider themselves introverts. Many prefer to work as helpers, not as leaders. Hope Scheele says she is most content to work in the background. Rachel Warner is more extroverted and loves to meet people. Fadia Jenkins prefers servant work that does not require leadership. God needs and uses all of us in different ways.

Paul wrote to the Corinthians that the body is not made up of one part, but of many.[58]

Now if the foot should say, "Because I am not a hand, I do not belong to the body," it would not for that reason stop being part of the body. And if the ear should say, "Because I am not an eye, I do not belong to the body," it would not for that reason stop being part of the body. If the whole body were an eye, where would the sense of hearing be? If the whole body were an ear, where would the sense of smell be? But in fact God has placed the parts in the body, every one of them, just as he wanted them to be.[59]

Some of us are tasked with being mouths. Some of us are tasked with being ears. Others are tasked with being hands. Only when we use our diverse gifts together can we be the body of Christ in the church. Paul wrote to the Ephesians, "From him the whole body, joined and held together by every *supporting ligament*, grows and builds itself up in love, as each part does its work."[60]

3. **Don't lose sight of your role in the family.** As you're finding your place in your new congregation, don't forget your critical place at home. Even as you work to build relationships with people in the church and in the community, you have precious relationships to tend to at home. These relationships, of course, are the most important ones to nurture. Tend to your

[59] 1 Corinthians 12:15-18
[60] Ephesians 4:16, emphasis mine.

the women I interviewed said that other pastors' wives from within their own district or circuit became their closest friends. These are women who understand and are living life as a pastor's wife in the LCMS. Because they are not directly associated with the church where your husband is pastor, they can be excellent and confidential sounding boards for issues or questions you have with your church.

4. **Don't be afraid to connect with pastors' wives outside of the LCMS.** One of my closest friends in St. Louis was my neighbor across the street, who also happened to be a Presbyterian pastor's wife. In Rapid City, I met and befriended the wife of a Christian Reformed Church pastor through my children's school. Many of the challenges, questions and joys we experience as pastors' wives in the LCMS are reflections of the challenges, questions and joys that pastors' wives experience in general. Just as my non-Lutheran pastor's-wife friends can relate to many of my questions and struggles and joys, I find I can relate to theirs.

5. **Be open to friendship in unexpected places.** Polly Rapp found a dear friend in the woman who taught her

piano lessons. "Often the lesson begins and/or ends with a chat about what's going on in our lives," Polly said. Two of Tess-Lynn Conklin's closest friends have been a Mormon bank teller and a Methodist Church secretary.

6. **Step outside your comfort zone.** Challenge yourself to push your own boundaries with how and where you meet people. "I'd give genuine compliments to a stranger or strike up a conversation with another mom at the playground," said Bethany Canaday. "I found that most people are really receptive to a stranger talking to them; they want to connect."

7. **Seek jobs that will help connect you to your community.** Debra Kinney got a part-time job with the local Chamber of Commerce. Her work put her in touch with business owners in the community who were not members of the church and who she may not have met otherwise.

children's needs before the church's needs. Tend to your husband's needs before the church's needs. When my husband tells me, "Our house could not run without you," I glow inside, because he is reinforcing the importance of my work at home. That work carries with it the most meaningful responsibility – caring for my family. No one else can care for and love my family like I can. No one else can care for your family and love your family like you can. Building and strengthening the relationships you have with your husband and your children in turn builds up the church, because it gives the church a healthier, more confident leader who has the energy and drive to love and serve its people.

The world turns on relationships. The church does, too. There's a good chance you'll always walk that fine line between being vulnerable (honest and open) and being protective as you navigate your relationships with others. As with everything, fall on grace. Pray for the people whose paths you cross, and don't be afraid to ask for prayer yourself. Love your husband, love your children, strive to love others, and practice wisdom in all your interactions. God will equip you. He gives you opportunities to practice all the time.

CHAPTER 15

Contentment and Sacrifice in the Church

As the pastor's wife, just when do you step into ministries of the church? At the seminary, you'll probably hear the advice to wait six months to a year before volunteering in any capacity. The idea is you want to really get to know the church you're serving before you focus your efforts and attention on any one area or ministry.

Some women are showered with requests and expectations to jump in with both feet the moment after their husbands are ordained and installed. Husbands and wives entering rural ministry might find they have to wear many hats, simply because there are not enough people to share the work of the church. Others, like me, feel on the fringes for a while. As the stereotype of "pastor's wife" is evolving, it seems a congregation's expectations of how pastors' wives should be involved in the church are changing, too. Generally speaking, most people understand that, like them, pastors' families have lives outside of the church building. Pastors' wives, like everyone else, are pulled in multiple directions: home, family, work, church.

I knew there were plenty of ways to get involved in my

new congregation, and I was eager to participate, but I wasn't immediately ready to jump in. What's more, no one in our church asked me to jump in right away. All in all, I believe this was the congregation's way of welcoming me and showing respect; people knew I would get involved when I was ready. Until then, no one was going to ask me to do anything.

Our congregation of three-hundred-plus active members had been operating with a single pastor for two years. With my husband's call and ordination came a wave of excitement and relief. It was palpable in the handshakes after service and in meals we shared together in fellowship. My husband was needed, and collectively, our family was needed. The gist I got overall was that the congregation would welcome my participation in anything any time I was ready to commit. But there was no pressure. My immediate call was to be present and supportive for my family. I knew there was a time to get more involved with the church, but I also knew it wasn't right away.

Like me, Hope Scheele felt the pulsing excitement of the congregation when her family arrived at Trinity Lutheran Church in Cortez, Colorado.

"It's safe to say that there were no expectations for me, at least that I'm aware of," she said. "They were just so excited to have a pastor again."

Several months into her husband's first Call in Sioux Falls, South Dakota, Liz Slavens, not having been aware of any expectations the church had for her, feared she wasn't doing enough. She sought the advice of the senior pastor's wife, who is heavily involved in church functions. The senior pastor's wife put Liz at ease. She assured Liz that the church has no concrete expectations of her and wanted to honor the fact that she was in the midst of raising four children. The senior pastor's wife only became more heavily involved with church ministries after her own children were older, she told Liz; she wasn't involved much when she was raising her own kids.

Erica McCarty said her congregation had expectations of her pretty quickly.

"But that was because, as my husband so lovingly says, I opened my big mouth and volunteered," she said.

Erica was eager to put her experience as a DCE to work in her new congregation. She volunteered to teach the Thursday morning adult Bible study, and she attends as many of the senior social gatherings as she can. Yet with young children, the time she is able to dedicate to church is still limited. It is important to her to help her husband, a sole pastor, as much as she can. But she also realized that sometimes the best way to support her husband is to take care of things at home.

"It's hard for me because I love being involved, but I think the church understands that in this season for us – for our family – it is better if I don't over-commit," Erica said.

These stories illustrate a wonderful truth about being a pastor's wife: most people today recognize that "pastor's wife" is but one role a woman who is married to a pastor has. That means that many congregations will patiently wait for the pastor's wife to grow into her role in the church and set her own expectations for how and where to be involved in the church.

The first time my husband approached me with a request to help at church was four months into his role as pastor. He was helping to lead a New Members' class, and most of the families had young children. He was looking for volunteers to assist with childcare during the classes, so that those families with children could still attend. When he finally asked me if I could help, the timidity of his request surprised me. Why did he seem so hesitant?

"I don't want to fall into that trap of assuming you're the obvious choice to help just because you're the pastor's wife," he admitted.

But truthfully, I was so excited that he asked me to help! For months I had been waiting for someone to ask me to help with something. There were plenty of opportunities to volunteer and serve, of course, but no one had approached me specifically with any requests. The first one to ask me to serve was my husband, and he made it sound as though I was the last person he wanted to ask. He was being protective of me. While I appreciated and understood that, I agreed to help right away. The choice for me was a no-brainer: I was helping our church by supporting the new members. I was supporting my husband. And, I was getting to know the newest children of our congregation and they were getting to know me.

Wherever you serve or choose not to serve in your new church, make sure you are filling yourself with God's Word regularly. A big reason why I tried to read the Bible from cover-to-cover while in seminary was to educate myself in Biblical knowledge, truth, and context. I wanted to be able to maintain theological conversations with my husband as he was growing and learning. I wanted to be confident in my own understanding of the Bible and history and not have to fall back on my husband every time I had a question.

Now that we are almost a year into public ministry, I realize another major benefit to steeping myself in the Word: I was – and am – preparing myself to be an encourager and a light to our congregation.

You are in a unique position as a pastor's wife to share in some major life moments with people in your congregation. Most likely, you will attend your fair share of weddings, funerals, and baptisms. One small way I saw I could love my congregation early on was by sending members cards for big moments. I know that one of my spiritual gifts is that of encourager, and I pray even now that God will use my small card ministry in mighty ways. One thing I realized as I began sending cards to congregation members is that Bible verses would pop into my head as I was writing. Alongside a prayer for comfort, I might jot down Psalm 3:5 – *I lie down and sleep; I wake again, because the Lord sustains me.* Alongside a message of encouragement I might share Hebrews 12:1-3 – *Therefore, since we are surrounded by such a great cloud of witnesses, let us throw off everything that hinders and the sin that so easily entangles. And let us run with perseverance the race marked out for us, fixing our eyes on Jesus, the pioneer and perfecter of faith. For the joy set before him he endured the cross, scorning its shame, and sat down at the right hand of the throne of God. Consider him who endured such opposition from sinners, so that you will not grow weary and lose heart.* These verses come to me by the Holy Spirit, Who blesses my time in the Word whenever I open my Bible. The more I read the Bible, the more I see God and His complexity. And the more able I am to see Him at work in my own life, my family's life and the life of the congregation. I want to be that fourth type of soil that Christ refers to in the Parable of the Sower in Matthew 13, the good soil that allows a seed to take root and produce a crop.

But how does soil become good? It requires regular tending. It requires water. And it requires light. We "tend" the soil by being in the Word regularly, and by watering our day-to-day life with the light of God's truth and promises. Being in Scripture enriches us, allowing the seed of the Gospel to produce "a hundred, sixty or thirty times what was sown" (Matthew 13:8).

One of the things the seminary warns about life in ministry is the sneaky temptation for pastors to put the church's needs above their family's needs. The church asks a lot of our husbands, and it is important that we give our husbands the space and peace of mind to care for their flocks in the myriad ways that being a pastor requires. Sometimes, the needs of the church will require priority over needs at home. Your family may have to adjust standard meal times to accommodate your husband's evening meeting schedule. Your husband might miss his son's baseball game because he is with a family whose loved one is in hospice. Your Christmas and Easter traditions will change with ministry, because, unlike many professions, these are two of your husband's biggest work days of the year.

It's when a pastor consistently puts the needs of his congregation over the needs of his family that Satan gains the upper hand.

"The temptation to prioritize ministry over family is not new," writes Brian Croft.[61]

What makes this tension between ministry and family so challenging is that caring for a congregation is a good thing. Pastors are needed on so many fronts, and the needs are always there. There will always be shut-ins who would love a visit from their pastor. There will always be congregation members facing surgeries or health difficulties who covet their pastor's prayers. There will always be facility issues to address, board members to chew the fat with, people in need. There will always be another church service to think about, another sermon to write.

"The problem rests not in the demands and pressures we face but in how we create idols out of those demands, idols that lead us to neglect our family and dishonor God," Croft writes.[62]

As a pastor's family, it is important that you draw the lines together of how your husband will respond to the needs of the church and how he is expected to still be the spiritual leader at home. Paul gives instructions to overseers and deacons in his first letter to Timothy, instructions that apply to pastors, as well: [The overseer] must manage his own family well and see that his children obey him, and he must do so in a manner worthy of full respect. (If anyone does not know how to manage his own family, how can he take care of God's church?)[63]

Ministry is a life of great sacrifice and great blessing. Because of the work of Jesus, sacrifice and blessing go hand-in-hand.

---

[61] Brian Croft and Cara Croft, *The Pastor's Family: Shepherding Your Family Through the Challenges of Pastoral Ministry*, 26.

[62] Brian Croft and Cara Croft, *The Pastor's Family: Shepherding Your Family Through the Challenges of Pastoral Ministry*, 49.

[63] 1 Timothy 3:4-5

One of the most valuable insights my husband gained from his four years at seminary was the realization that many things in life are held in a paradoxical tension. As Christians, we are both sinners and saints, for example. We are free in Christ even though we are slaves to sin. I recognize another tension now with my husband as pastor. As a pastor's family, we are held to a higher standard than the average family. Yet we fall short all the time. As a pastor, my husband is held to a higher standard in how he conducts himself in thought, word, and deed. Brian Croft writes that "Pastors need to remember that God has established a high standard for those who shepherd his people in terms of how they live out their calling as a husband and a father."[64]

Yet my husband is still human.

I was not prepared for the frustration and disappointment that bubbled up in me whenever my husband found himself in a valley. Moments of anger seem angrier than they did prior to his work in the ministry. Moments of doubt seem more desperate. I want him to be stronger than anger. I want him to rise above doubt. I want him to overcome weakness.

I know he is held to a higher standard in the church. But I did not expect I would hold him to a higher standard as his wife, at home. Was that fair?

Therein lies the tension. On one hand, he is a leader, a role model to whom people should be able to admire. On the other hand, he is just as much a sinner and just as imperfect as the rest of us. My husband has enough stigma placed on him outside of his family in his public role. Shouldn't his home be a safe place where he can let his demons out, rather than one more place where they are not allowed?

Brian and Cara Croft encourage: "As you put off your sin and put on Christ, remember that the fruit of God's work in your

---

[64] Brian Croft and Cara Croft, *The Pastor's Family: Shepherding Your Family Through the Challenges of Pastoral Ministry*, 26.

life, the things that first qualified you for pastoral ministry must continue to be evident, not just to your church, but to your wife and children as well."[65]

What qualified my husband for pastoral ministry to begin with? I believe it was an insatiable thirst to know God more and to dig into the rich theology behind who our Triune God is. My husband felt at home in church. He felt invested in his church far more than in his professional role as an engineer. But none of that made him a super-human.

The aim of a pastor and a spiritual leader is always to draw closer to God. The closer one gets to knowing God, the harder Satan is going to fight to wrench that focus away. When you're doing amazing things for the kingdom, Satan will try all the more to interfere.

Paul encountered interference in his ministry often. He suffered time and again for the Gospel. He was imprisoned, flogged, and often near death. He survived no fewer than three shipwrecks, and at least one changed the course of his ministry. He was hindered from seeing the Thessalonians.

Yet, in all of his suffering, Paul boasted. He boasted not in his strengths, but in his weaknesses. Why? Because he knew God was working through them. As in Paul's case, it may well be that setbacks and weaknesses actually equip your husband for pastoral ministry. Think back to the Bible stories you know. How often does God use the most unlikely people to accomplish His will? Gideon was a farmer who God called to be a military commander. His army of just three hundred men defeated tens of thousands of Midianites.[66] David was a shepherd who became one of Israel's greatest kings. He slayed a giant with a single stone. Moses clearly lacked leadership qualities, yet God called him to lead a nation,

---

[65] Brian Croft and Cara Croft, *The Pastor's Family: Shepherding Your Family Through the Challenges of Pastoral Ministry*, 54.
[66] See Judges chapter 7.

anyway. Many of God's prophets did not see their divinely inspired messages accomplishing anything. But God called them to be faithful, reassuring them He would take care of the results.

God shines in the ordinary and the mundane of life. Time and again, Jesus used the ordinary as a platform for teaching. He uses shepherds, fathers, sparrows and blades of grass to teach us about His love for us.

He uses ordinary men like our husbands to shepherd His people.

Psalm 15 asks, "Lord, who may dwell in your sacred tent? Who may live on your holy mountain?"[67]

"[He] who keeps his oath even when it hurts."[68]

By using the most unlikely people for His work, God reveals His glory. He reminds us that all glory belongs to Him – Sustainer, Provider, Protector – and that with Him, all things are possible. In her book, *Making Room: Recovering Hospitality as a Christian Tradition*, Christina Pohl writes: "Israel's identity as chosen by God yet alien in a land reinforced the necessary relationship of dependence and faithfulness, gratitude and obedience."[69] By working through us despite our frailties and failures, God shows us over and over how His power is made perfect in weakness. Sometimes God strips us of what we think we need, so that when provision comes, all we can do is point to Him.

"Your ministry and family are not designed by God to take from one another, but rather to enhance one another," Pastor David Sunday writes on The Gospel Coalition website.[70] "You

---

[67] Verse 1a

[68] Verse 4b

[69] Christina Pohl, *Making Room: Recovering Hospitality as a Christian Tradition* (Eerdmans, 1999), 28.

[70] David Sunday, "Embracing the Biblical Tension Between Family and Church Ministry," The Gospel Coalition, May 15, 2012, https://www.thegospelcoalition.org/article/embracing-the-biblical-tension-between-family-and-church-ministry/.

do not separate your life as a husband and father from your life as a pastor—-in fact, you believe that through your ministry as a husband and father, God is using you to shepherd your church, and through your shepherding of the church God is equipping you to build up your family."

What a beautiful and noble relationship to be a part of! God uses our families to help build up the church, and He uses the church to help build up our families.

Another tension that comes with being a pastor's wife is a tension of belonging. On one level, you are a member of the congregation. The church your husband pastors is your church, just as it is the church of every other member. As a church member, you should feel at home in the church. You should feel welcome. You should feel wanted.

Yet as pastors' wives, we can never simply be church members. We cannot separate our vocation of "church member" from our vocation of "pastor's wife."

The uniqueness of the pastor's wife role causes many women to carefully consider various ways to be involved in the church. Should you join a church board to better get to know the inner workings of the congregation? Or would joining a board be a conflict of interest? Is it more important to get a pulse of the church through involvement on a board, or stay out of board involvement completely so that you don't make your biases known? Would joining a board hinder other board members from being completely candid, because the pastor's wife is present?

At a PALS retreat during my husband's first year of ministry, I asked fellow pastors' wives if any of them had joined a church board. I was wrestling with these very questions. I had sat on a variety of church boards over the years as a church member (not wife of the pastor), and I was always amazed at the insight into the health of the congregation I gained by participating in board meetings. As a church member, I had come to believe that there was no better way to get to know a congregation than to join a board. I also felt that it was part of my duty as a member of the congregation to serve in an area that could particularly use my God-given gifts. But that was as a church member. Were there other things I should consider as a pastor's wife before jumping right in to a particular ministry of the church I really cared about?

None of the newer pastors' wives at that PALS retreat had joined a board. It turned out they had the same questions I had. One of the more seasoned pastors' wives in our group shared her own story of being invited to sit on a board. Once she joined, she began to wonder whether she was asked to be on the board because she was the pastor's wife or because of her own identity apart from that as pastor's wife. As discussion and differences in opinion sometimes arise during church meetings, she questioned whether her involvement on a board could be considered a conflict of interest. While she knew she was welcome to serve on a church board, just as anyone else in the congregation, she struggled with this notion of whether it was a good idea or not. Eventually, she was honest with the other board members and politely stepped away.

Another pastor's wife shared with me that she served on a board early on in her husband's ministry. The president of the board asked her to broach some sensitive subjects with church staff members, because she was the pastor's wife and the staff would therefore listen to her. The board president saw the opportunity for a favor from the pastor's wife because of her position within the church. He took advantage of that, even though it was not the pastor's wife's responsibility to bring up those subjects with the church staff.

I am learning that we can't ever simply be church members or board members or servants of the church. We will always also be pastors' wives. Of course, this doesn't mean that we can't or shouldn't be involved in ministries of the church. There is no "right" way to be a pastor's wife. Using your God-given talents for the church can be a beautiful and God-honoring goal. Because of their location, their size, their history, etc., all churches have different needs. But I am coming to understand that a pastor's wife must approach opportunities to be involved in the church with a heightened discernment. And we can't be effective or influential if we don't first take time to get to know and understand the congregation.

Another facet of congregational life that many pastors' wives approach with careful consideration is voter's meetings. As a church member and as the pastor's wife, do you vote on key issues of the church? On one hand, you are a member of the church and you have just as much say in decisions of the church as any other member. On another hand, can you fairly express your concerns and positions on issues without creating conflict? And can you handle tensions in the event a meeting evolves into a heated debate?

In an informal poll, I posed this question to the Wives of LCMS Pastors Facebook group. The responses illustrate just how complex this issue is. More than 100 LCMS pastors' wives weighed in on the question of voting. Of those who responded, just shy of half attend voter's meetings and vote. About thirty-eight percent do not attend and do not vote – either by choice, or for logistical reasons such as a job conflicting with the meeting time or no childcare being offered at the meeting. A small faction of respondents attend meetings but do not vote. For another small faction, the decision to vote depends upon the church's dynamics. Finally, three percent belong to churches where only males are allowed to vote.[71]

This poll showed how varied women's thoughts and emotions are when it comes to church voter's meetings. Below is a sampling of perspectives:

---

[71] Women's suffrage was not granted in the LCMS until 1969.

"I vote. I'm too involved not to."

"By attending, you get to know the dynamics of the congregation and what is important to them."

"I, personally, will always want to attend. How much I contribute depends on the stage of life and importance of the issue."

"I attend and vote. In 15 years, I've only spoken once."

"I found it was easier for me to love people, my husband and the church if I wasn't aware of all the nit-picking, personal attacks, etc."

"I don't attend or vote. This way I don't take anything personal against my husband or me. I can love every member regardless of votes. It works for me."

"It would be too hard to hear any complaints or criticism that may come out and not take it personally."

"I am a voting member of the congregation. My husband just happens to be the pastor."

"It's good for me to hear what's going on, and if there's any criticism, they should be able to say it in front of me."

"I felt it was my church and I should do what was expected of every other member."

"I asked my husband. He wants me to go, so I do."

"I find it helpful to go and listen to see who needs encouragement and who needs help. We are at a large parish and school so I'm not always aware of what's needed, besides prayer."

Our roles as pastors' wives look so different, from one congregation to the next, from one community to another and from one woman to another. Because no two churches are alike, there are few strict guidelines for the involvement of a pastor's wife in her church. This makes the fulfilling of our vocations as pastors wives complex and not very clear-cut. To live out our roles well, we can only turn to Jesus in prayer.

In his exposition of Psalm 147 in 1531, Martin Luther wrote: "Labor and let Him give the fruits. Govern and let him give his blessing. Fight, and let him give the victory. Preach, and let him win hearts. Take a husband or a wife, and let him produce the children. Eat and drink, and let him nourish and strengthen."[72]

As pastors' wives, it is both our privilege and our responsibility to give to our congregation. But giving can be expressed in many different ways. Your giving may be front-and-center, leading or directing a particular ministry of the church. Your giving may be from behind the scenes, quietly supporting your husband from outside the church's walls. You will likely have to experiment to find your sweet spot in your church's ministry. How you serve in one congregation may not make sense for a congregation that calls your husband down the road. I am finding that my role in the church is an iterative process. That means that through prayer and action, I move forward, always knowing there is grace if I feel led to shift course. When I feel called in a particular direction (to volunteer with a particular ministry, for example, or take the lead on something), I pray. I talk to others about that direction. I seek my husband's input. Then, I either move forward, or I don't. Congregation members may understand your involvement or lack thereof in the church, and they may not. Either way, your service and your heart toward the congregation, your husband, and your family is a matter between you and God.

Cara Croft writes that ministry is a way of life requiring us to constantly pour ourselves out for others. As pastors' wives, we should expect to give sacrificially of our time, resources, and emotions. In the midst of challenge and heartache, triumph and joy, we see God at work. We gain a front-row seat to the amazing miracle of God's love working on and for the people in our midst.[73]

The view from my front-row seat is dynamic and mostly beautiful, and I am honored to occupy that place.

---

[72] *Luther's Works* 14:115.
[73] Brian Croft and Cara Croft, *The Pastor's Family: Shepherding Your Family Through the Challenges of Pastoral Ministry*, 68.

CHAPTER 16

Faith in Your Role in the Church

"What fills the space
from here to the horizon?"

-Jeffrey Brown, "Cortona"

You are a pastor's wife now.

But that's not the end of the story.

"Pastor's wife" is one vocation to which God has called you. But it's not your only role. It's not even your number-one role.

Who are you in Christ? That's your most important role.

For many women, that question of "Who am I" is split wide open in the transition from seminary into a husband's first Call. Doors that may have seemed closed for a time are suddenly flung open again. You look at your surroundings from a new perspective. Everything around you is new. And it is yours to explore.

Anna Davis had many ideas of what she had to offer, both within and outside the church, during seminary – ideas that she felt she could not pursue in that temporary season. Once her husband began serving as a pastor full time, she allowed herself to start getting excited about possible opportunities she herself could pursue. She was interested in becoming a post-partum doula. But she was also interested in serving as an at-home educator for younger children or owning a creative space that would bring people together to experience community in different ways. While Anna has not pursued any of these ambitions yet, she is giving herself permission to dream.

Rachel Warner knew that marrying a pastor would likely mean she would have to give up her beloved job as an architect, because she would be moving to rural Arizona where her husband was called. As far as she knew, there were no architecture jobs in the small town they would soon call home. As she made the move and began to settle into their new apartment, anxiety welled up in her. Rachel was an extrovert; she needed to be out in the community, doing something. She applied to be a delivery helper for UPS during the holidays. Then, she found a job at a Hallmark store. She continued to look for work in her trained field, and in the meantime, she had a place to be each day, where she was surrounded by people and where others depended on her. Eventually, she found a job in architecture she could do remotely. Working from home has been an adjustment, she said, but she gets her people fix by taking her work to a local coffee shop one or two days a week.

Haley Albright worked as a speech pathologist for twelve years before marrying Matt Albright shortly after he graduated from seminary.

"I love my job," Haley said. "It's part of who I am."

Even as she and Matt were married and prepared to settle down in a new community in a new state, Haley was determined not to let go of her vocation as a speech pathologist. She would get licensed and find work in Minnesota, where Matt was called. Coming to terms with leaving the job she loved in Missouri and having no guarantee of when she could pick up that work again was the hardest part of marrying a soon-to-be pastor.

As I look at the trajectories of the lives of the women I interviewed for this book, very few women launched into new ambitions immediately after settling in their new community. Growing accustomed to a new place takes time. Many women continued the important work they were doing at the seminary – raising children. Others, like Leslie Barron and Heidi Bentz, continued in the careers they pursued while their husbands were in seminary. Still others took on jobs not out of career ambition but strictly for financial reasons.

In the LifeWay Research survey conducted in 2017,[74] sixty percent of women reported that the compensation paid by the church isn't enough to support their family. That means many families must find other ways to make ends meet.

Anna Davis designs costumes for the theater department at the local Lutheran high school and works part time as a teacher's aide at the same school her children attend.

"It's not something I see myself doing forever," Anna said, "but having a schedule that matches the kids' and a director that is very understanding has made it a very good solution for the time being."

When her family moved to Milbank, South Dakota, following four years at seminary, Pam Vogel took a part time job in the custodial department at the local cheese factory. She intentionally sought work that was not emotionally taxing, so she could still be fully present for her family of five kids when she was home.

Even if God does not open doors right away (or the doors that you want Him to open), take heart that He is using you right where you are.

God does not promise perfect balance in this life. You may take on a job, only to realize it is not a good fit for the family

[74] LifeWay, "Pastors' Spouses Experience Mixed Blessings."

dynamics you are working to achieve. You may pray for direction, only to find that God is telling you to stay right where you are for now. Less than a year into her family's move to southern California, Michelle Knauss was still trying to find her place. She asked herself where she might best serve in the church, and whether she should go back to school.

"I feel like I hear God really telling me to be wife and mom and not to focus on all of the other things right now," she said.

That statement was true a year later, almost two years into her husband's pastoral role.

"I continue to pray for God to lead me where He wants me and for me to be content where I am," she said. "I will always pray for God to open new doors for me to learn and serve His people."

You may find that God leads you through a financial valley for a while, challenging you to trust Him to provide. You may find He provides in ways you did not expect. One of our parishioners brings by boxes of ground beef every so often. Because of him, we have not had to buy beef at the store for almost a year.

I love what Luther says about the connection between our work and God's design of creation:

As referenced in Robert Kolb's and Charles P. Arand's *The Genius of Luther's Theology*, Luther writes:

> For God rules us in such a way that He does not want us to be idle. He gives us food and clothing, but in such a way that we should plow, sow, reap, and cook. In addition, He gives offspring, which are born and grow because of the blessing of God and must nevertheless be cherished, cared for, brought up, and instructed by the parents. But when we have done what is in us, then we should

entrust the rest to God and cast our care on the
Lord; for He will take care of us.[75]

The work that we do as women is no less important than
the work our husbands do as church leaders. Carrying out the
mundane and ordinary tasks of life is part of our walk of faith.
The tendency to desire work that is extraordinary and exciting is
not new. By striving for rigorous devotion and religious tasks, the
monks of Martin Luther's day neglected the necessary everyday
tasks at hand. Luther criticized these monks for failing to recognize
these ordinary tasks as work that God ordains.

Kolb and Arand write that faith "embraces the most menial
activities, for God's Word has given them his stamp of approval.
These are the very things he wants us to do. For this reason Luther
constantly chose ordinary activities from daily life as examples of
a Christian's return to creation and embrace of vocation."[76]

I'll admit I had big ambitions when our family left seminary
and headed west for South Dakota. We had moved to St. Louis for
my husband to start seminary just as I felt like my own career as
a writer and editor was starting to gain some traction. For years
I had stayed at home with our two boys, learning to navigate the
world of parenthood even as I questioned time and again whether
I was cut out for it. I wondered day in and day out how I could
weave my writing and editing work into this full-time parent
lifestyle. After years of trying, tweaking and trying again, I had
finally found that "sweet spot" – a routine that allowed me to both
stay at home with my young children and live out my God-given
vocation as a writer.

But all of that was dependent on my husband's paycheck.

When he went to seminary, his paycheck went away.

That meant I couldn't continue to stay at home with our kids

---

[75] Kolb and Arand, *The Genius of Luther's Theology*, 122 (see also *Luther's Works* 8:94).

[76] Kolb and Arand, *The Genius of Luther's Theology*, 112.

and write. We needed more money coming in, and together, we decided that meant I needed to work full time during the years he was in school.

To me, that meant putting my writing/editing career on the back burner.

So after Call Day came and went and we were on our way to a new place where my husband would start his new full time career, I had to remind myself not to get carried away dreaming of the possibilities. The excitement of what could be pulled at me like an eager child. Now that we would be settled, I could have a writing studio! I could develop a regular clientele and writing schedule! I could launch the writing workshops I had taught prior to seminary!

God had to pull me back down to earth. I am writing again regularly, and I am picking up editing clients slowly. But settling into a new place, a new life, a new normal, takes time. My husband had to remind me how the traction I had gained as a writer prior to seminary was a multi-year process. Success and realized dreams would not happen overnight. And even as those dreams are ever-so-slowly taking shape, still God calls me to the ordinary tasks of life: caring for our home, picking up boys from school, driving them to practices, planning and preparing meals. Furthermore, He has called me to this new role of pastor's wife. What does that look like, exactly?

I am learning that being a pastor's wife comes with its fair share of contradictions. You are simultaneously well known and anonymous. Almost everyone knew me by name at my husband's ordination. Hardly anyone called me by name in church the following Sunday. It might be difficult, at least early on in your husband's ministry, to assert your own identity as a woman with a first name. You are more than pastor's wife, but it might take congregation members some time to get to know you as a person, beyond that role. That is totally normal.

Your role as a pastor's wife may be a rich connecting point for some and a turning-away point for others. One thing I learned early on in my position of pastor's wife is that I have many simple opportunities to talk about spiritual things with a lot of different people.

Bethany Canaday, a pastor's wife in Spencerport, New York, told me that one of the challenges she has come up against is when people ask what her husband does.

"When I mention he's a pastor, some people clam up, shut down/put up walls, clean up their language, tell me they really need to get back into church or start confessing," she said.

First Peter 3:15 says to "always be prepared to give an answer to everyone who asks you to give the reason for the hope that you have."

I bumped up against this verse time and again throughout our years at the seminary – and then after my husband was ordained. I wanted people to know that my husband was a pastor, but I didn't want that fact to stand in the way of people being themselves around me. At the same time, I didn't want the fact that my husband was a pastor to influence people's perception of me – or my husband or my children.

"Oh! I better watch what I say!" the father of a boy on my son's flag football team said after we had introduced ourselves. "You're the pastor's wife!"

A spear of annoyance shoots through me any time I hear something like this, because I want people to feel comfortable around me. I don't want people to feel like they have to put up walls. Yes, I am the pastor's wife. But I am also entirely human. At the end of the day, we are just people – imperfect and broken – like everyone else. If anything, I long for that badge of "pastor's wife" to be an invitation for people to connect with me, rather than a wall that turns people away.

Another contradiction that comes with the role of pastor's wife is that you are simultaneously strong and vulnerable. Your family is a pillar of the congregation. People look to your husband as a leader, and your husband looks to you for support. You want to hold him up, and you want to support the church and its ministries where and when you feel led. At the same time, because you are a pillar of the congregation, you are prone to easy criticism.

We can't deny the fact that pastors – and pastors' families – are held to a high standard when it comes to the way we conduct our lives. This is evident in both the big and the small moments of life. In the 2017 LifeWay Research survey, eighty-six percent of respondents believed that the pastor's marriage should be a role model for members of the congregation to shape their own relationships.[77] The thought of my marriage being a role model for others is for me a tremendous honor. At the same time, it can also be intimidating! Bryan and I have our touchy moments, just like everyone. We don't see eye-to-eye on every single thing. We are best friends – but even best friends have heated words now and then.

But all in all, I believe our marriage is a stronger role model because it is not perfect, not because it is perfect.

Perhaps this is also why I generally don't get anxious over knowing that people are watching us, as a pastor's family. Maybe because I'm a writer who loves sharing real stories, I see this "spotlight" as more of an opportunity than as a threat. Being a pastor's wife is certainly not an opportunity to model perfection; rather, it is an opportunity to model grace in imperfection. I want to be myself with people, and I want people to be themselves with me. That desire would exist in me whether I was a pastor's wife or not.

Most of us probably know the idea of the "Proverbs 31 woman."

"Her children arise and call her blessed; her husband also, and he praises her …." (31:28)

The textual note on this verse in my Bible explains "blessed"

---

[77] LifeWay, "Pastors' Spouses Experience Mixed Blessings."

as "one who enjoys happy circumstances and from whom joy radiates to others."

I want to be that woman. But I don't want to be that woman because I am a pastor's wife. I want to be that woman because of what Christ did for me on the cross.

As Lutherans, we profess "faith alone." But James tells us that faith, when it is strong and vibrant, is fueled by works.[78] We can't help loving and serving when we realize the extent to which God loves us. We want to treat people the way God treats us. We want to love people the way God loves us. We know we can't. But it doesn't mean we don't try.

As I continue to navigate my personal and professional roles in this new place, I pray I can model the Christian attitude that Kolb and Arand so beautifully describe: "As [Christians] strive to do their best in the various roles they find themselves, they let God crown their efforts with success when, where, and how he sees fit."[79]

Above all, my role in the church is to love. But yet again, that would be true whether I was a pastor's wife or not. I want to love my husband as his number-one supporter. I want to love my children because God has entrusted them to me. And I want to love the people in my congregation, because He has placed me in their lives and them into my life. I want to love all of these people when it's easy to love them. And I pray for the Lord's help to love them when they are difficult to love. Because I am human and also broken, I pray that the Lord will help others to love me, too, especially when I am difficult to love.

Pam Vogel said she has seen her own mindset change in her time both at and since the seminary.

---

[78] See James 2:18. A text note on James 2:14-26 says that people are justified (declared righteous before God) by faith alone, but not by a faith that is alone.

[79] Robert Kolb and Charles P. Arand, *The Genius of Luther's Theology*, 122.

"My identity is definitely more in Christ and less on my abilities," she said.

When I think about what a stereotypical pastor's wife was one or two generations ago and compare that to pastors' wives I know now, a lot has changed. Yet for some reason, that stereotypical image of a pastor's wife remains the same. Expectations and stereotypes of the pastor's wife are part of the history of the church. But rarely have I encountered expectations or stereotypes in my own brief tenure as a pastor's wife, apart from the expectations I have put on myself. By and large, I believe a pastor's wife today has a lot more space to be herself, with less assumptions from others weighing her down.

When you think back to pastors' wives of past generations, what immediately comes to mind? For me, it is the super-involved woman with lots of children at her feet who cooks for the congregation and plays the organ and teaches Sunday school. It's safe to say that nearly all of the women I interviewed for this book would classify themselves as a "non-typical" pastor's wife. But if none of us is the "typical" pastor's wife, what even is typical in our current age?

"I am so far from the traditional pastor's wife," said Leslie Barron. Leslie classifies herself as independent and opinionated. "I don't sing. I don't teach. I'm not a nurse. I don't play the piano. I practice Jujitsu."

She is also a government contractor with top secret security clearance.

Katie Schultz was raised by a single mom and did not grow up in the Lutheran church. She has a lot to learn still about Lutheran theology.

Kristin Bayer plays the saxophone – not the organ.

What about you? What sets you apart?

The roles and expectations of pastors' wives are changing, and overall I think that is a good thing. Women who faithfully follow their husbands into the ministry by and large encounter churches that have less defined expectations of them, which means they allow us more freedom and grace.

Let's take advantage of that freedom to be our unique selves – the shining lights that God calls us to be in our various ways. And let's drink in God's grace to show our congregations that we are human, just like them, and we are imperfect, just like them, and we depend on God's forgiveness and mercy, just like them.

"Pastor's wife" is a part of your story now. But it is not the be-all end-all of who you are. The more comfortable I grow in the role of pastor's wife, the more I see that it's a role meant to complement – not govern – every aspect of my life. I serve. I love. I write. I say "yes" to some opportunities and "no" to others. I play baseball with my kids. I love alternative music from the nineties. I drink lots of coffee and I love a glass of wine. I am four years into my two-year plan to read the Bible from cover-to-cover. I have never touched an organ. I have never made a Jell-O salad for a potluck, and I probably never will.

I am a pastor's wife. I am a mom. I am a writer.

But more than all of that, I am God's child.

Remember how God sees you. He calls you by name (Isaiah 43:1). He calls you beloved. You belong to Him.

STUDY GUIDE QUESTIONS

The questions that follow are meant to give the reader further opportunity to reflect on the book's content, chapter-by-chapter. The questions are intentionally broad, and suitable for individual study, journal reflection and/or group discussion.

CHAPTER 1: WRESTLING WITH GOD
THROUGH THE DECISION

1. Read Exodus 3:1-4:17. How would you describe the voice of God in these verses? How does Moses respond to God? Why do you think Moses is so hesitant?
2. Did you or your significant other struggle with knowing the voice of God as you were contemplating seminary? What was that process like?
3. In what ways does God speak to you? How did He lead your significant other/you/your family to the seminary?
4. Did you resist the possibility of seminary at first? Why/why not?

CHAPTER 2: COMMUNITY IN THE DECISION

1. What questions did you face (both as an individual and as a family) as you prepared to come to seminary?

2. Once you/your family made the decision to come to seminary, did you come right away, or did you wait? What factors influenced the decision of *when* to come to seminary?
3. What did you look forward to in coming to seminary? What did you lament leaving behind?
4. Hebrews 11:1 defines faith as "confidence in what we hope for and the assurance of what we do not see." With this definition of faith in mind, read Hebrews 11. Make a list of the Bible names the chapter mentions and the specific act of faith for which each is credited:

Person from the Bible	Act of Faith
Abel	Brought better offering to God

CHAPTER 3: CONTENTMENT AND SACRIFICE IN THE DECISION

1. Have you ever encountered a time when you felt comfortable and content, only for a major change to rock your world? If so, talk about where you were comfortable and what impending change rattled your comfort zone.
2. Did your husband resist the call to ministry at first? Why/why not?
3. What things/people/dreams/ideas did you have to let go of to come to seminary?

4. Why should we ever turn our backs on comfort, stability, even a sense of permanence — all seemingly good things — to leap into the unknown?
5. Look at Exodus 3:11-12. How did God respond to Moses' question, "Who am I that I should go …?"
6. Read John 14:15. How does this verse speak to your current situation? Where do you particularly need to obey God right now?

CHAPTER 4: FAITH IN YOUR ROLE THROUGH THE DECISION

1. What is it about the term "pastor's wife" that causes so much angst?
2. List some areas where you feel you fall short, areas in your life where you don't feel you are "enough." Read or take turns reading the following Scripture passages:

   - 2 Corinthians 3:5
   - 2 Corinthians 12:9-10
   - Romans 3:23

   Talk about or reflect on how each verse addresses the notion that you are not enough.
3. Talk about your own experience of coming to the seminary. How did your family dynamics change? What in your family dynamics remained the same?

CHAPTER 5: WRESTLING WITH GOD AT SEMINARY

1. Name some words that you associate with transition. Discuss with others what brings these particular words to mind.

2. Did you struggle with resentment or self pity when you came to the seminary? Why/why not?

3. What (if any) roadblocks or hesitations did you encounter in coming to seminary?

4. What excited you about seminary and the transition there?

5. In Luke 1, God sends angels to two people with two similar messages. Read Luke 1:1-38. How does Mary's response to the angel differ from Zechariah's response to the angel? Why do you think God imposed consequences on Zechariah?

6. In what ways did the move to seminary challenge or change your family dynamics?

7. Read 1 Timothy 6:7. Nothing belongs to us – not our homes, not our jobs, not even our children. Everything belongs to God. How does this truth encourage or challenge your perspective of seminary and what comes after it?

CHAPTER 6: COMMUNITY AT SEMINARY

1. Is it worthwhile to make friends, knowing that seminary is only a temporary stop? Why/why not? Is this a question you have considered on your own journey?

2. What do you look for in a friend?

3. Have you encountered any creative ways to meet people, whether in your own experience or in witnessing someone else's experience?

4. Have you gotten to know anyone else's faith story on campus? If not, make it your goal to do that this week. Ask one person about their faith walk. See where the conversation leads. You might start with the question, "What brought you to seminary?"

5. Think about the people you've met at the seminary. What are some common traits you are finding in the people you meet here?

6. What communities other than seminary are you a part of right now? Where among these communities do you feel led to exercise and share your gifts?
7. If you were to choose one thing – one way to be involved, or one relationship to pursue – right now, what would it be?

CHAPTER 7: CONTENTMENT AND SACRIFICE AT SEMINARY

1. By coming to seminary when you did, what did you say *Yes* to? What did you say *No* to?
    I said "Yes" to ...
    I said "No" to ...
2. What is God saying "Yes" to in your life and in your family's life right now? What is He saying "No" to?
    God is saying "Yes" to ...
    God is saying "No" to ...
3. Read Hebrews 13:5. Did you or do you struggle with a love of money?
4. Hebrews 13:5 tells us to be content with what we have. In what areas of your life are you content right now? In what areas do you struggle to be content? Where do you most need to trust God right now? In what area of your life do you most need to trust that He will never leave you?
5. What were the advantages and disadvantages you foresaw in coming to the seminary? What issues or things did your family have to seriously consider if seminary were to become a reality?
6. Have you played the "What-if" game at seminary? *What if God calls my husband to Alaska? What if my kids don't grow up near their grandparents? What if we spend two decades of our lives in a parsonage?* If you have played this game, what "what-if" questions have crossed your mind?

7. Balance is not only the woman's struggle at the seminary; it is also the man's struggle. Men must weigh their academic responsibilities and any extra job or work study with family time. How do you feel your husband is balancing his own priorities, between academic course load, work and family time?

8. What gesture of service has blessed you most as a family at the seminary? The Adopt-A-Student program? The Re-Sell-It Shop? The Food Bank? Something else?

9. Is accepting help or support from others difficult for you? Why/why not?

CHAPTER 8: FAITH IN YOUR ROLE AT SEMINARY

1. Describe the trajectory you are on as an adult, and how seminary has influenced that trajectory. Are you a new wife working in your first full-time job? Are you a stay-at-home mom who continues to stay at home during the seminary years? Are you a retired professional who is working part-time while your husband is in school? Where does seminary fall on your life's journey?

2. Reflect on your identity before coming to the seminary and now at seminary. What parts of your identity have changed, and what has remained the same?

3. Does what you do = who you are? Why/why not?

4. When you think of the term "pastor's wife," what comes to mind? Describe pastors' wives you have known (if any). Is "pastor's wife" a role you look forward to? Why/why not?

5. God makes each of us different and desires to use us in different and various ways for His glory. Read Romans 12:4-8. What gifts has God blessed you with? Do you see a place or an opportunity to use those gifts in your

current surroundings? Do others recognize potential opportunities for you to use your gifts?

6. Psalm 138:8 reads, "The Lord will fulfill His purpose for me; your steadfast love, O Lord, endures forever. Do not forsake the work of your hands." In what area of your life right now do you most need the comfort this verse provides? Which of the three parts resonates with you most?

- The Lord will fulfill His purpose for me
- … your steadfast love, O Lord, endures forever
- Do not forsake the work of your hands

Prayer: *Dear Lord, help us to see our work as a gift from you. Amen.*

CHAPTER 9: VICARAGE: A BIRD'S EYE VIEW

1. What factors are important to your family (husband/children) when considering the type and location of church your hopes to serve?
2. What factors are important to YOU when considering the type and location of church your family hopes to serve?
3. What new thing do/did you most look forward to, anticipating your husband's vicarage year?
4. What is one thing that you dreaded or that made you nervous, anticipating your husband's vicarage year?
5. Chapter 9 brims with questions to consider for the vicarage year. Skim the chapter. Underline (and share) one or two questions that resonate with you.

CHAPTER 10: GETTING INVOLVED ON VICARAGE

1. Have you thought about how you might want to be involved in the congregation where your husband will serve as a pastor? Talk (or write) about your thoughts on this.
2. Spend some time this week praying for God's direction for you during vicarage year, the year of practical application. In a journal or notebook, reflect on where or how you feel God is leading you. Is He asking you to be involved and immersed in the congregation? Is He encouraging you to take a step back and observe? How might He be working?
3. My key word for vicarage year was "observe." What might your key word be?
4. What does/did God *not* expect of you during vicarage year?
5. If you chose just one thing to be involved in during vicarage, what would it be?
6. Read Ecclesiastes 3:1-8. What verse speaks to you most in your current moment?

CHAPTER 11: FROM VICARAGE TO CALL

1. Name one way that vicarage helped to equip your family for pastoral ministry.
2. Did your vicarage experience bring any new insights or considerations into what type of a congregation dynamic best fits your husband and your family?
3. Think about the "goodbyes" that capped your husband's vicarage year. Which "goodbyes" were the hardest? Which were the easiest?
4. Think back to when you first set foot on the seminary campus. What didn't you know at that time that you know now, about life in ministry?

CHAPTER 12: IDENTITY IN THE CALL PROCESS

1. Read Romans 8:28. To what purpose is your husband being called? To what purpose are you being called? In what ways do you see God working for the good of you and your family, "who have been called according to his purpose?"

2. God doesn't require us to have a specific skill set before He calls us to a role. Look at 1 Corinthians 4:2. What DOES God require of us?

3. What does it mean to you to be "open" to where God is leading? How do you think being "open" is connected (if at all) to the desires of your heart – to where you truly want to be?

4. Where we come from and who we come from in part define us. These details in part make us who we are. Reflect on those pieces of your identity. How did where you come from and who you come from inform your journey through the seminary and/or into life in the parish where your husband serves?

5. "To be" is the infinitive of "You are." What does God say about "you are?" Look at the following verses: Genesis 1:27, Psalm 139:13-14, 1 Corinthians 3:16, 2 Corinthians 5:17, Ephesians 2:10, 1 Peter 2:9

6. Read Luke 5:1-11. Imagine you are Peter. How would you respond when the nets start to break and your boat starts to sink? Would you respond any differently than Peter did? Why or why not?

7. Read Psalm 16. What stands out to you according to your circumstances right now? Where in this chapter do you find the most comfort?

8. Make a list of your current roles – wife, mother, daughter, home owner, apartment renter, etc. Then, circle the roles that might change when your husband receives his first Call. How many of your roles will NOT change?

CHAPTER 13: WRESTLING WITH GOD AFTER THE CALL

1. Make a list of who you are: wife, daughter, etc. What has life at seminary taught you about who you are – and who you are not?

2. In the days following the Call announcement, what do/did you know about the church where your husband was Called? What questions about the church and/or your husband's position linger(ed)?

3. During our transition from the seminary to the parish where my husband was Called, God worked on my humility. In what area of your life might God be working on you right now?

4. What things were easy to let go of from the seminary years? What things were not so easy to let go of?

5. Read Proverbs 19. What words or phrases of wisdom stand out to you, in this current moment?

6. Having your heart in multiple places is hard and beautiful. Where is your heart right now? Read Hebrews 13:8 and Isaiah 40:8 and take comfort in our unchanging Father.

7. What are some advantages of transition and starting over?

8. Do you have any stories about connecting with other congregation members in their vocations outside of church? For example, have you sought an oil change from a mechanic who belongs to the church, or daycare services from someone in the church who runs a daycare?

9. Where do you go for services such as a doctor's visit, dentist or counselor? How did you make these types of connections in your community when you needed them? Does your position in the church influence who you reach out to for certain services? Why/why not?

CHAPTER 14: COMMUNITY IN THE CHURCH

1. Have you received support or blessings from unexpected places during your husband's tenure in the church?
2. In what ways have you gotten to know members of the congregation your husband serves?
3. Did you branch out or have you branched out in effort to get to know people in your community who are NOT part of the congregation? If so, how did you engage these people?
4. Were you interested in meeting/connecting with people outside of the church? Why/why not?
5. Did you have a best friend or close friends during your time at the seminary? Consider reaching out to someone who you were close with during the seminary years. Who would it be?
6. Do you see yourself as a fixer? Explain your answer.

CHAPTER 15: CONTENTMENT AND SACRIFICE IN THE CHURCH

1. Read 2 Corinthians 12:9. Identify some weaknesses that you and/or your husband have. Where might Christ be working in your or your husband's weaknesses right now?
2. Think back to when your husband first started seminary. What qualified him for pastoral ministry? Do you see those same qualifications, now that he is a pastor? Do you see other qualities you didn't recognize before or qualities he has developed since being at the seminary?
3. Were you concerned about the impact that being a pastor's family would have on your children? If so, what were some of your fears or apprehensions? Now that your husband is in the ministry, do you see any of those fears becoming

reality? How have your children processed and adjusted to the role of "pastor's kid?"

4. How are you filling yourself with God's word regularly?

5. Balance between church life and home life is one of most common struggles for pastors and their families. How do you see this balance playing out in your family?

6. As a wife, how do you respond to your husband when he fails to rise above anger, doubt or other weaknesses?

7. Read 2 Corinthians 11:16-33. What does Paul say about the many hardships he endured?

8. Think about the tension of belonging as it relates to your role in the church. Do you feel this tension at work anywhere? Why/why not?

9. As a pastor's wife, do you attend and/or participate in church voter's meetings? Why/why not?

CHAPTER 16: FAITH IN YOUR ROLE AS A PASTOR'S WIFE

1. List the positive and negative aspects of the circumstances God has allowed in your life at this time. How can God use your life – good and bad – to show His presence, love and grace to those around you?

2. What part of the transition to being a pastor's wife took (or is taking) the most time for you adjust to?

3. List what you think might be some reasonable expectations a church has for a pastor's wife and some unreasonable expectations. What makes the reasonable expectations reasonable and the unreasonable ones unreasonable?

Reasonable	Unreasonable
To see you in church on a regular basis[80]	To have a long and involved conversation about church matters in the middle of the grocery store
To trust that you will pray for your congregation and its individual members, with or without request	To relay a critical message to your husband (Hey, tell Pastor to call me because I want my granddaughter to be baptized)
To relay a non-critical message to your husband (Please tell Pastor that I loved his children's message last week)	

4. This chapter points out some contradictions that come with being a pastor's wife. For example, you are simultaneously well known and anonymous. You are simultaneously strong and vulnerable. Have these contradictions been true for you? Have you noticed any other contradictions that come with your unique role?

5. How do you find people respond to you when they learn you are the wife of a pastor? Do people seem to be more open to conversation or less open, or does the fact that you're a pastor's wife have little bearing on how they interact with you?

---

[80] Most pastors lead more than one church service each week, whether a result of serving a dual parish or offering multiple services over a weekend. So it is not reasonable for people to expect to see you at the exact same time and place every week, but it is important that you maintain a regular presence.

6. When you think of the stereotypical pastor's wife, what comes to mind? Why?
7. Do you consider yourself a typical pastor's wife? Why/why not?

BIBLIOGRAPHY

Croft, Brian and Cara Croft. *The Pastor's Family: Shepherding Your Family through the Challenges of Pastoral Ministry.* Zondervan, 2013.

Fryar, Jane. *Today's Light* 21, no. 4 (2016) Dec 7.

Goehmann, Heidi. *The Mighty & The Mysterious: A Study of Colossians.* St. Louis: Concordia Publishing House, 2019.

Heintzen, Erich. *Prairie School of the Prophets: The Anatomy of a Seminary 1846-1976.* St. Louis: Concordia Publishing House, 1989.

Kolb, Robert and Charles P. Arand. *The Genius of Luther's Theology: A Wittenburg Way of Thinking for the Contemporary Church.* Baker Academic, 2008.

LifeWay Research. "Pastor's Spouses Experience Mixed Blessings." September 12, 2017. https://lifewayresearch.com/2017/09/12/pastors-spouses-experience-mixed-blessings/.

Meyer, Carl S. *Log Cabin to Luther Tower: Concordia Seminary During One Hundred and Twenty-Five Years, Toward a More Excellent Ministry 1839-1964.* St. Louis: Concordia Publishing House, 1965.

Pohl, Christina. *Making Room: Recovering Hospitality as a Christian Tradition.* Eerdmans, 1999.

Weaver, Joanna. *Having a Mary Spirit: Allowing God to Change Us from the Inside Out.* Waterbrook Multnomah, 2006.

INDEX

A

Aarsvold, Melanie 81
Adopt-a-Student 21, 208
Adopt-A-Student 69
After the Boxes are Unpacked 70, 148
Arand, Charles P. 194, 195, 199

B

Barron, Kevin 6
Barron, Leslie 27, 38, 139, 193, 200
Bartok 115
Bartok, Jim 19, 115
Bartok, Kim 19, 70, 115, 150
Bartok XE 156
Bayer, Kristin 3, 64, 70, 125, 134, 200
Bayer, Tim 3
Bolosan 3
Bolosan, Chad 9, 37, 44
Bolosan, Sherry xix, 37, 41, 44
Brakhage, Joshua 135
Brakhage, Suzy 40, 70, 135, 149
Brandmahl, Ashley 29, 30, 53
Brandmahl, Josh 30
Bridgman, Adam 7, 156
Bridgman, Julie 119, 156
Buvinghausen, Emilia 45

Buvinghausen, Garrett 45

C

Canaday, Bethany 176, 197
Concordia Publishing House 13, 49, 108
Conklin, Tess-Lynn 176
Croft, Brian 13, 24, 182, 183
Croft, Cara 13, 190
Cullen, Kimberly 86, 87

D

Davis, Anna 20, 119, 133, 166, 191, 193
DeMeritt, Beth 161
DiLiberto, Anthony 80
DiLiberto, Jamie 66, 80, 125, 130, 155

F

Fink, Kelsey 11, 12, 57, 83, 141, 149, 160, 165
Fink, Sam 11, 17
Fryar, Jane 38

G

Garcia, Chris 11

Garcia, Liz 11, 19, 26, 83, 123, 143, 155, 159, 167, 169
Geraci, Coleman 44
Geraci, Rachel 44, 52, 141
Gibbs, Renee 69, 73, 74, 84, 123, 148
Goehmann, Heidi 5, 56, 60, 160, 170
Gradberg, Kim 57

H

Harrington, Melissa 135
Haupt, Celina 26, 72
Highley, Joseph xvii
Highley, Rachell xvii, 43
Hileman, Christina 44, 47, 135
Hileman, Josh 19

J

Jander, Coreen 6, 9, 23, 41, 58, 66, 135
Jander, David 6, 9, 23, 66
Jenkins, Fadia 8, 51, 77, 84, 174
Jenkins, Jeff 8, 77
Johnson, Kara xvii, xx, 57, 67, 77, 86, 87, 118, 124
Jones, Beth 57, 86

K

Kegley, Beth 62, 67
Kinney, Debra 176
Knauss 68
Knauss, Matt 8
Knauss, Michelle 8, 20, 54, 63, 73, 133, 168, 169, 194
Knutson, Nicole 174
Kolb, Robert 194, 195, 199
Kubowicz, Nikki 161

L

Lamie, Juli 42, 52, 79, 147
Lamie, Julian 7
Larson, Eric 44
Larson, Judy 44, 79
LifeWay Research 165, 193, 198
Luther, Martin 3, 128, 141, 163, 189, 194, 195

M

Magill 18
Magill, Mary 18, 118
Magill, Timothy 17
McCarty, Erica 21, 27, 37, 42, 46, 64, 82, 124, 134, 148, 165, 179
McCarty, Nate 42
McGinley, Gretchen 53, 127, 143
McGinley, Kelsi 38, 56, 73, 77, 118
McGinley, Michael 3, 38
Meier, Beth 20, 54

N

Nehring, Joe 7
Nehring, Linda 144

O

Okubo, Debbie 174

P

PALS 172, 174, 186, 187
Peter, Dr. David 138
Price, Jenny 9, 23, 59, 78
Price, Nick 59, 78, 79

R

Rapp, Polly 175
Rodriguez, Adam 40
Rodriguez, Kyla 40, 124, 146
Roll, Latashia Lynne 25

S

Scheele, Hope 64, 119, 123, 174, 178
Schuetz, Christine 56
Schultz, Katie 40, 54, 85, 200
Slavens, Doug 115
Slavens, Liz 115, 169, 178
Sunday, Pastor David 185

T

Terral, Jamie 53, 68
The Gospel Coalition 185
Today's Light 13

V

Vogel, Josh 6, 19

Vogel, Pam 19, 54, 70, 81, 126, 193, 199
Voskamp, Ann 72

W

Wallace, Diana 174
Warner, Daniel 148
Warner, Rachel xvii, 148, 165, 169, 174, 192
Weeks, Krista 40, 51, 54, 116, 142, 150
Weeks, Kyle 40, 116, 142
Wendorff, Aaron 39, 43
Wendorff, Leah 39, 43
Widener, Amy 85
Will, Amy 149
Wrede, Bill 17
Wurm, Kyra 167

Z

Zech 54, 55
Zech, Melissa 10, 12, 20, 21, 38, 54, 70, 142
Zech, Rako 10, 12, 38

ABOUT THE AUTHOR

Kate Meadows is a pastor's wife, mother of two, and writer/editor/ writing workshop instructor in Rapid City, SD. Her husband, Bryan Meadows, graduated from Concordia Seminary in 2019 and serves as Associate Pastor at Zion Lutheran Church in Rapid City. Kate earned her MFA in Professional Writing from Western Connecticut State University in 2010. Since then she has published a collection of essays, Tough Love: A Wyoming Childhood, and numerous articles and essays in national, regional and local publications. A native of Wyoming, she was raised in the LCMS church. www.katemeadows.com